WHO WROTE THE CLASSICS?

WHO WROTE THE CLASSICS?

Volume I

Nora Stirling

ILLUSTRATED BY EMIL WEISS

THE JOHN DAY COMPANY

NEW YORK

The John Day Company, 257 Park Avenue South, New York N.Y. 10010
An Intext Publisher

Fourth Impression

Published on the same day in Canada by Longmans Canada Limited.

Library of Congress Catalogue
Card Number: 64-20698

MANUFACTURED IN THE UNITED STATES OF AMERICA

Contents

WILLIAM SHAKESPEARE
9

JANE AUSTEN
29

NATHANIEL HAWTHORNE
51

EDGAR ALLAN POE
73

CHARLES DICKENS
99

THE BRONTËS
117

JULES VERNE
145

MARK TWAIN
169

ROBERT LOUIS STEVENSON
191

RUDYARD KIPLING
219

BIBLIOGRAPHY
247

To
Christopher and Audrey Vandercook

William Shakespeare
(1564=1616)

William Shakespeare

(1564-1616)

WILLIAM SHAKESPEARE, surely the greatest writer the world has ever produced, is, in his own person, one of the least known. The facts about him are so scarce not because he lived four centuries ago, but simply because he was a man of the theatre. In those days no one connected with the theatre was considered worthy of a biography.

Not until thirty or forty years after his death was a biography attempted. By then all those who had known William Shakespeare personally were dead, and the writers had to scrape together a hint here and a court record there, building on these scraps their own conjectures with which to flesh out the meager story. More of these conjectures piled up over the years, many gradually becoming popular myths and in time taking on the stature of solid fact. It is still possible, however, by clinging to early records, to separate the facts from the myths.

One of the indisputable facts is that Stratford in Warwickshire was Shakespeare's birthplace. This pretty town sat amid farming country, with the Avon flowing through it and the Forest of Arden nearby. In his time it was a medieval community with a council that enforced the laws strictly; if a man's duck wandered or his children stayed out after eight, he was heavily fined. But Stratford was a bustling and prosperous place, and a certain forward-looking farmer settled there about 1550.

9

John Shakespeare, William's father, went into the glove-making business and, as a public-spirited citizen, became successively ale-taster, alderman, constable, town chamberlain, and High Bailiff, the town's first officer. Just as important to his future, he married Mary Arden, daughter of a family in which had been Lords of Warwick since William the Conqueror's day. Mary brought John Shakespeare considerable wealth, and he acquired three tall-gabled houses on Henley Street, one of which he rented out while the others, thrown together, became the Shakespeare home. There were barns and gardens and orchards, and Master John was an imposing citizen. He even dreamed of some day becoming a gentleman.

This was no matter simply of deportment and appearance. England's population was divided into four ranks—peasants, yeomen (farmers), gentlemen, and nobles—and the lines between were as cut-and-dried as those of a modern army. Yeoman John Shakespeare, aspiring to move up one rank, applied to the Office of Heralds for a coat of arms, and for a while his prospects appeared good, for a design was drawn for him. Then for some reason—the records are tantalizingly blank—his social rise halted. He stopped attending council meetings and retired from public life. The guess is that he suffered some personal embarrassment, for soon afterwards he borrowed a sum of money, and several lawsuits over property were recorded. The coat of arms did not eventuate, and instead of John Shakespeare, Gentleman, he remained plain Master John Shakespeare.

Meanwhile, the children had been arriving. The first two were girls and they died early. Then, in 1564, there was a boy. And here, at the very outset, one of the myths falls apart. April 23 is called William Shakespeare's birthday, but only his baptism on the 26th was ever recorded. However, since baptisms followed births by two or three days and because England's patron saint George was born on April 23,

SHAKESPEARE

(from the Droeshout engraving, 1623)

William Shakespeare

Shakespeare's worshipers later thought, What a nice coincidence if his birthday had been the 23rd too! Gradually the wish became the fact. Actually, nobody knows.

The baptism, however, was carefully documented. John Shakespeare being town chamberlain at the time, the Church of England ceremony took place in the handsome old Church of the Holy Trinity before godparents and a congregation, with Vicar Bretchgirdle officiating.

After William came three more boys, Gilbert, Edmund and Richard, and two girls, Joan and Anne. Having learned the rudiments of reading, writing and the catechism from the parish clerk, the boys—though perhaps not the girls—entered the Stratford grammar school at the age of seven. They attended every day in the year except Sunday from seven till five, and learned Latin—reading, writing and reciting Latin— and almost nothing else. No mathematics, no history, no science, no geography, and no other languages except, occasionally, ancient Greek. There were no dictionaries, and everyone made up his own spelling—even his own words if he felt the urge. All practical knowledge was picked up outside. But by the 1580's, when young Will Shakespeare was growing up, the eager English mind was becoming impatient of this antiquated school system, and books and pamphlets on a great variety of subjects were being published in London.

Stratford, it is true, still lacked these luxuries, but it did afford other pleasures to its young folk. Great fairs were held every spring and fall, bringing crowds to town and, to entertain them, circus acrobats, performing animals and clowns. Twice a year, acting companies toured the provinces under the patronage of some court nobleman whose prestige assured them a place to put on their plays. As son of the High Bailiff, young Will must have seen many of these performances.

This is conjecture, for nothing positive is known of his

life until November 17, 1582, when one William Shagspere applied for a license to marry. (Names were written as they sounded, and some of the spellings of this one—Shaxberd, Shaxpeare—suggest that it was pronounced differently in his time.)

Anne Hathaway, eldest daughter of a landowner in nearby Shottery, was eight years older than her eighteen-year-old bridegroom, William. This fact, together with the birth of Susanna six months later, has been taken to suggest a marriage of necessity. But by the laws of the period, a betrothal or "precontract" was legally binding, and any offspring was considered legitimate. In 1585 there was another baptism, this time of the twins Hamnet and Judith. After this, his name disappears from the records for seven years.

There are, to be sure, plenty of myths to fill the gap, myths which arose long after his death. He has been variously assigned careers as a schoolmaster, an apothecary, a dyer, a notary, a printer, a soldier, a horse-tender for theatregoers, and one diehard tradition has him arrested for poaching on the estate of a certain Sir William Lucy.

All these tales are later additions, however, and the next unquestionable fact is that by 1592 he was a resident of London and already well known as an actor and the author of three or four plays. Reason tells us that this could not have been accomplished overnight, so the inference is that he left Stratford soon after the birth of his younger children, the twins.

Anne had not followed him to London, nor ever did. Her family were Puritans, and it was probably Puritan dislike of his disgraceful profession rather than indifference to her husband that caused the estrangement. For judging by others' comments, Will Shakespeare was a man of most extraordinary charm. He was "handsome and well-shaped"; he was "gentle," "courteous and honest." His colleagues men-

14

tion his friendliness and witty conversation. Taking his own gifts in stride, with relaxed good humor, he never displayed the temper misnamed temperament, and he was a man deservedly known to his friends as "Sweet Will."

Shakespeare was fortunate in the times in which he lived. Two centuries earlier, in Geoffrey Chaucer's day, writers had been restricted by the Church's disapproval of love stories and dramatic realism, and fifty years later Puritan austerity again closed down. But for a brief sunlit span Shakespeare's genius could blossom in freedom, and it was even encouraged by the theatre-loving Elizabeth and her successor, James I. England was just then bursting into new life, exhilarated by the explorations of Raleigh and Drake and Frobisher and the recent victory over the Spanish Armada. The world overseas displayed intoxicating possibilities, and everyone was feeling a little drunk.

Moreover, men's minds were swinging open to new knowledge. Other subjects than Latin were being taught in London's schools—law, medicine, music, geometry, rhetoric. Books were being read by the thousand. For daily news, large sheets of paper, called broadsides, were sold in the center aisle of St. Paul's Cathedral between services.

Contrasted with Stratford, London must have seemed like a continuous fair to the enterprising young stranger. There were zoos and circuses, complete with freaks, cockfights and bear-baitings, and public hangings at which the modishly dressed criminals gave stirring farewell speeches. There were Queen Elizabeth's processions through the city in red velvet and gold, with twenty-four maids riding behind her in single file. And best of all, there were the theatres.

This was a new development. Until recently there had been no real theatres; plays had been put on in the rectangular courtyards of inns, with the actors working in the open air on a raised scaffold. Part of the audience stood on the ground at their feet (hence the name "groundlings"), while the more prosperous sat in the windows of the inn. But in 1576 an actor in the Earl of Leicester's company, James Burbage, put up a building especially to accommodate his plays. Burbage went to the outskirts, across the open fields, and the theatre he erected was round, with a stage jutting out in the center. The seats around the sides were thatched over and the stage was roofed, but the penny groundlings still took the rain on their heads.

The horrified Puritans preached against these "sinks of theft, pride and prodigality, villainy and blasphemy," but all of London, men and women, boys and girls, flocked there for two hours of excitement under the afternoon sun. By 1585 a second theatre was in operation, then a third and a fourth. But none prospered like that of Burbage, whose son Richard was the greatest actor of the age. (There were no actresses, all female roles being played by boys.)

The drama of the day was of two different kinds. One harked back to the Greeks and Romans—Seneca, Sophocles, Plautus—and stuck close to their pattern, all dialogue in rigid iambic pentameter verse, and all action kept decorously off-stage. It took a university education just to master the rules of composition.

The other kind was all passion and pageantry right before one's eyes, battles with fencing and stabbings all marvelously real. Limbs were strewn about the stage exuding sheep's blood (oxblood was too thick and wouldn't run), and for a disemboweling the liver and lungs of a sheep were tucked into the actor's tunic, to spurt out at the touch of a dagger. The Devil erupted from hell with real fireworks; an angel descending from heaven, or Jonah leaping from the whale's belly, was not beyond these accomplished stage mechanics. It was all strictly for the masses, and writing for this theatre Marlowe, Jonson, Kyd, Greene, Nashe, Shakespeare and Hey-wood reveled in its freedom and let the intellectuals go hang.

There was little money in it, however, and less fame; a script was sold outright for six or eight pounds and was printed anonymously if at all, for the author's name was of no interest to anyone. Financial rewards and fame were found only in acting, and it was as an actor that Shakespeare won his. It was his acting, too, that taught him how to write for actors.

Since the company's repertory was constantly adding new plays, the actors were always rehearsing as well as performing. Rehearsing, Shakespeare learned the practical as well as the artistic side of his trade—what the voice and body could do most effectively. Performing, he learned what made audiences laugh and weep. He observed the sharpness of their imagination and put it to work, letting a couple of torchbearers suggest a street corner and a group carrying napkins a banquet hall. He trusted his audiences' imaginations, and they never failed him.

From the start he cared for nothing but to please the common people. Since England's history was not taught in schools and her people had a vast curiosity about their own past, he gave them history, *Henry VI, Parts 1, 2 and 3*. Although he used Holinshed's *Chronicles of England, Scotland and Ireland* as his source, he was wildly inaccurate, misdating Joan of Arc by twenty-two years. Moreover, his demands were somewhat impractical, calling for severed heads brought in on trays and a cast of fifty characters for a dozen actors to play. But he had the feel of drama, and already the audiences were enchanted.

For a while he imitated others: *Titus Andronicus* tried to be a noble history in the classic style, but it was his melodrama and poetry that the English liked. *A Comedy of Errors* was a stab at an Italian classic farce, and *Love's Labor Lost* was a parody on the word-play and sonnets fashionable at the time. However, these plays had so firmly established him as a playwright that by 1592, when his name appears again in the records, he was a popular success in a very low-class field.

At this point the plague struck London. The helpless public looked everywhere for the cause of these periodic visitations of death, but the clergy knew whom to blame. "The cause of plagues is sin," they thundered. "The cause of sin is plays; therefore the cause of plagues are plays." This was unanswerable logic, and every theatre in London was shut down for nearly two years.

For actors there was only one recourse, touring the country towns. But this was only possible in good weather and in the winter Shakespeare had time on his hands. For an energetic young man whose livelihood was cut off, there remained nothing but to try another field. Now, perhaps, was the time to make something of himself, to rise above his low beginnings and prove himself a real artist. Poetry was the language of the intelligentsia, the longer and more formal the better, so young Master Shakespeare composed a narrative poem on a Roman theme.

A publisher was found for *Venus and Adonis* through friends, and since every book had to have an aristocratic patron, he looked around for some titled gentleman—not necessarily one he had met in person—to dedicate his to. A favorite patron of struggling poets was the young and rich Henry Wriothesley, Earl of Southampton and Baron of Tichfield. One poet had recently implored him in print: "Vouchsafe to sweet it with thy blessed tongue / . . . So shall my tragic lays be blest by thee / And from they lips suck their eternity." Another's dedication hailed Southampton's "gracious eyes, those heavenly lamps which give the muses light," and still another, "the glorious and gracious sunshine of your Honor." The Earl was indeed young and handsome and rich, but one wonders if he was as heavenly as all that.

In any case, what was good enough for others was good enough for Will Shakespeare, and the nineteen-year-old earl was subjected to yet one more eulogistic dedication. This of Shakespeare's actually was quite restrained, merely expressing the hope that the poem would please his Lordship and apologizing for the presumption of choosing "so strong a prop to support so weak a burden." He called his poem "the first heir of my invention," disregarding his plays, for of course plays were not thought to be in the same class with poems.

Venus and Adonis was a runaway success, going through ten editions, and Shakespeare immediately followed it with another stylish effort, *The Rape of Lucrece*. The earl seems to have responded to the first dedication satisfactorily, for the second crawled with gratitude and "love." Then, according to the best guess, came the Sonnets.

These poems, not to be compared in quality with the plays, have received disproportionate attention because of the autobiographical clues they offer to Shakespeare's private life. Actually, the solid facts they supply are few in number, and even these have been inflated and distorted by Shakespearean scholars ever since. These few facts are: the Sonnets, when published, were dedicated to "Mr. W.H."; many were addressed in highly charged words to a handsome youth, some of them imploring him to marry and perpetuate his beauty; others were addressed to a "black mistress"; a few were to unidentified persons.

From the tone of those to the "black mistress" (whom later scholars have sentimentally renamed the "dark lady") one infers that she was the great, destroying love of Shakespeare's life, whom he adored and yet whose character, whose very appearance, he despised. They show him racked by jealousy and despair. It would seem he could not forget her, for his plays abound in references to black eyes and black brows and black hair. But all attempts to identify her are guesses and no more.

The handsome youth is likewise impossible to name positively. The Earl of Southampton and the Earl of Pembroke have both been nominated on the thinnest of evidence, Pembroke because after Shakespeare's death a collection of his plays was dedicated to him, Southampton because of the fulsome dedications in *Venus and Adonis* and *The Rape of Lucrece,* and both because they had, in some combination, the initials W and H. Such evidence has been interpreted by some as proving that Shakespeare loved Mr. W.H., whoever he was, with an abnormal passion.

This assumption ignores the common speech of the time, which was generally more ornate than today's. "Love" was the usual word for friendship between men, and carried no further connotation. Ben Jonson, for example, called Shakespeare "my beloved," and no one suspects Jonson of abnormality. Altogether, the scantiness of facts has driven Shakespearean scholars to extremes of speculation, and one must finally settle for enjoying his work on its own merit.

It is known that many of the sonnets were written while Shakespeare was sitting out the plague, but in 1594 the quarantine was lifted and the theatres were reopened. By now his two long poems had established him in the fashionable literary set and he might have continued in it indefinitely, but his dramatic urge was too strong, and when he could, he returned to his proper niche, the theatre.

The company he joined now was under the patronage of the Lord Chamberlain, who was the Queen's cousin and a person high at court. It was headed by Richard Burbage, England's greatest actor, and made up of talented and dedicated men. Though actors were traditionally "rogues and vagabonds," not so "The Chamberlain's Men." They were respectable family men, homeowners and taxpayers; Shakespeare soon became a partner and he acted with them and wrote for them, day in and day out, for sixteen years. The world is fortunate that he had such a congenial instrument to play upon.

Performing and rehearsing constantly, he still turned out two or three or four plays a year, writing as naturally as a stream flows downhill. He knew that his scripts would be cut to two hours' playing time during rehearsals, and so, trusting his colleagues' judgment, he did not bother to hold back the flow. The words poured out in an ecstasy of creation, the clean, unblotted manuscripts revealing how few changes he had to make.

It is true he seldom invented new plots, borrowing not only from Holinshed's *Chronicles* but from the plays of other authors. But this did not matter; the glory of his poetry and the richness of his characterizations were something entirely new, and he could take a hackneyed story such as *Romeo and Juliet* and make of it something startling in its vitality. In the next years he wrote *The Taming of the Shrew* (was he vicariously taming his own unmanageable Black Mistress?), *A Midsummer Night's Dream*, *Richard II* and *The Merchant of Venice*, all plays of a rosy complexion by a romantic young man.

Through the 1590's his popularity increased steadily. His name was actually being attached to the published texts of his plays—and to some by other men too, to make them sell better; and though he always lived in plain lodgings, he was moving in glittering circles. The Chamberlain's Men played annually at Court, opening their season the day after Christmas before that avid playgoer, the Queen. Shakespeare was of course never really accepted by the nobility, but he mixed with it on a semi-friendly basis, like that of court clowns or exotic pets, and his contacts may have facilitated the happy ending to his father's search for gentility. For in 1592 a new draft for a coat of arms was approved and John Shakespeare became a gentleman.

Next year the Shakespeare family advanced still farther up the ladder. The actor son bought New Place, the second largest house in Stratford, which brought with it such prerogatives as a special pew in church. The actor was becoming a man of substance.

In 1599 The Chamberlain's Men opened a fine new theatre,

the Globe, and here *Julius Caesar* was first presented, followed by a series of light romantic comedies. In several of them one sees Shakespeare's rebellion against casting the women's parts with males; he always kept his female characters to a minimum, and often made a virtue of necessity by having them dress up in men's clothing.

About this time a change of mood is noticeable, as when a bright day clouds over. The essential man does not change, but a darkness creeps over him. No one knows the cause, though there are many theories. His only son and cherished heir Hamnet had died in 1596. The prosperity of his acting company was for a time threatened by a rival group. There was political turmoil at Court and some of his personal friends seem to have been involved. But these alone do not seem sufficient cause. There is no documented evidence to explain the trend from comedy to tragedy, and some scholars say it was not outside influences at all, but his own deepening sense of the tragedy of life.

Hamlet appeared in 1601, a study in revenge, indecision and "internal darkness." It is by far the longest of the plays and contains the largest vocabulary, reflecting Shakespeare's fondness for inventing colorful words. As originally written it had to be drastically cut to fit the two hours' playing time, but in those days there were no intermissions and the actors spoke very rapidly, so that not much was lost to those alert audiences.

He had, as usual, taken a shoddy old melodrama for his plot. But the story was not what made *Hamlet* the most popular play ever written. It is the one play that strikes home to every man, for Hamlet, like every man, is brave and cowardly, courteous and rude, intelligent and superstitious, loving and vicious. He is above all bewildered, and who is absolutely sure of anything in this world?

The next several years were filled with such a press of work that the mind boggles in contemplating it. Not only were there the lesser works such as *All's Well That Ends Well* and

Measure for Measure, but *Othello, King Lear,* and *Macbeth,* in which he reaches sublime heights of poetry, comprehension and grandeur.

There was, inevitably, a decline then to more earthly levels, broken by the towering love story of *Antony and Cleopatra,* which must have severely strained the capacities of the boy cast as Cleopatra. About this time Shakespeare made one puzzling descent into such a pit of blackness that some scholars attribute it to a nervous breakdown. *Timon of Athens,* a study in hatred, appears to be a deliberate stab at a play in one mood, but the careless writing suggests that he had soon lost interest and dropped it after the first draft.

In 1608 the Globe was closed again "for the plague." When it reopened, seven of the company, including Richard Burbage and Shakespeare, took over the fine new Blackfriars Theatre and there presented the last group of plays. *Cymbeline, A Winter's Tale* and *The Tempest* suggest the calm and serenity of prosperous old age, and though in 1610 Shakespeare was only in his middle forties, he seems to have worn himself out. He had continued buying up property in Stratford, and now he retired to live with his family, a landowner with a coat of arms.

With the death of his son he had lost all hope of keeping his name alive, for he had only daughters left. Still, they might at least provide him with a grandson. With this thought in mind he wrote a most careful will, leaving his whole estate to that possible heir, except for the customary third to his wife. As a man of property he had a certain claim on local remembrance, though none, of course, as an actor or scribbler of plays.

He had still not lost touch with London, however, having bought a piece of property near the Blackfriars Theatre. It is not known whether he was present at the première of his last play, but one rather hopes he missed that afternoon's catastrophe.

By 1613 Queen Elizabeth was dead and James I was king.

Henry VIII had been written to glorify the birth of Elizabeth, and on the stage the coronation of her mother, Anne
Boleyn, was a dazzling pageant in which the actors wore
replicas of the original royal robes. Fireworks heralded the
entrance of Anne, and though fireworks had been used in
plays for years, this time they happened to fall on the
thatched roof of the theatre and set it ablaze. In a few hours
the famous Globe Theatre was no more.

No one knows the cause of his death, which took place on
April 23, 1616. Only fifty-two, he hoped till the end that one
of his daughters would preserve his memory through a male
heir named after him. Neither did, and his carefully treasured
estate went to a granddaughter; after her time it was broken
up. Thus he was left with nothing to save him from oblivion
but a few plays.

As a respectable member of the Stratford church, he was
buried inside its chancel, and his epitaph reveals how deeply
he was concerned for his afterlife. It was common practice
to dig up old bones to make room for new, and Shakespeare
did his best to protect his own from such paltry treatment.
The epitaph read: *Good friend, for Jesus' sake forbear / To
dig the dust enclosed here. / Blest be the man that spares
these stones / And curst be he that moves my bones.*

A few years later a statue was placed over his grave. It was
a stiff carving in painted limestone, with hazel eyes, auburn
hair, scarlet doublet and black robe. There is in it little sug-
gestion of a living person. Probably the best likeness of him
is the Droeshout engraving included in the first complete
edition of his plays.

With Richard Burbage's death in 1619, the only two men
left of the original company were John Heminges and Henry
Condell. They had loved Shakespeare like a brother, and
now they collected into one large volume the various versions
of the thirty-six plays hitherto published individually. This
First Folio contained many typographical errors, for no first-

class printer would be bothered with such material, and it found a place in the Oxford University library only because the printer customarily sent to the library one copy of everything he turned out. For the two actors such a venture was expensive and risky, but their love for Shakespeare was well repaid—the book sold immediately and a second edition was required within ten years.

Because in those days books needed the greatest send-off possible, the Earl of Pembroke and his brother were enlisted as patrons. Four poets also contributed verses of commendation, of whom only Ben Jonson was well known. His literary standing was loftier than Shakespeare's for he had had a university education, and he could not resist a sidelong swipe at his friend's "little Latin and less Greek." But the poet in him was forced to recognize the playwright's greatness, and he well knew that such genius required no help from schoolmasters. William Shakespeare was, in effect, not an "Elizabethan poet" at all, nor an "English poet," nor even an "English man." He was poetry itself, man himself, and would endure as long as they both endured.

Jane Austen

(1775–1817)

Jane Austen
(1775-1817)

O<small>N</small> M<small>ARCH</small> 14, 1826, Sir Walter Scott noted in his diary:

> Read again for the third time at least, Miss Austen's finely written novel of *Pride and Prejudice*. That young lady had a talent for describing the feelings and characters of ordinary life which is to me the most wonderful I ever met with. The big Bow-wow strain I can do myself like any now going; but the exquisite touch which renders ordinary things and characters interesting is denied to me. What a pity such a gifted creature died so early!

Nearly a hundred and fifty years later Jane Austen is still the envy of other writers. And among readers she has a cult loyal to the death. The Jane Austen Society meets to collect and preserve mementos and information about her, and a "Janeite" will purple and explode if anyone suggests she is less than perfect.

But Jane is tantalizing, for most of her life is an enigma—not because she was herself enigmatic, but rather because she was so simple and normal. No one who knew her suspected she was a genius, so for fifty years after her death there was no biography of her, and the only portrait extant is a sketch by her sister Cassandra.

This life, in truth, contained little to record, no travels—

she was never farther than a hundred miles from home—no struggles, scandals or catastrophes. Obscure she lived and nameless she wrote, and fame crept up on her slowly, reader by reader. It is said the happiest individuals are those without a history, for history prefers catastrophes, and by this standard certainly Jane qualifies as a happy person. Hers was the grace of spontaneous joy; she once said, "I am not one to wait for enjoyment until there is some opportunity for it." Personal tragedies did occur or she would not have been human, but she did not brood or wail. And since no well-bred woman carried on in public about her woes, there is scarcely a trace of the tragedies in her work.

Some writers' books are nothing more than autobiographies, written to relieve the authors themselves; others aim to teach or reform. Jane did neither. She did not even try to entertain, for entertainment implies a performer and an audience. She simply wrote to please herself, letting her exuberant spirits gambol where they would and standing aside to look on with amusement. Of course, she liked the praise and the "pewter," as she called money, but they were not her goal.

Hers was an auspicious background for a writer—clergymen, lawyers and professors, with a salting of titles and neither too much money nor too little. Soon after her father, the Reverend George Austen, and Miss Cassandra Leigh married in 1764, they moved into the rectory at Steventon, a village in the balmy south of England. He preached on Sundays, tutored boys on weekdays, and drove a handsome carriage and pair, while she ran the household and produced a crop of eight children.

Though it was the custom to board out each new baby with a wet nurse for a year or so, the Rectory's three sitting rooms and seven bedrooms were still crowded. But the establishment was a happy one; Mrs. Austen was lively and easygoing, the rector was genial, and as the family increased,

JANE P. AUSTEN
(after her sister Cassandra's watercolor)

the warmth thus put into the house and the resulting fun made it a gracious place.

The Austen children were generously endowed. Although one little boy died in babyhood, the other five grew up healthy, handsome, and, judging from their later careers, brilliant. James went to Oxford and then into the church. Edward, especially beautiful and winning, caught the eye of the very rich relatives Mr. and Mrs. Thomas Knight who, themselves childless, begged the Austens to spare them this one boy out of their plenitude. He was legally adopted and in time inherited Godmersham Park and Chawton Manor.

Henry, the handsomest and most versatile of the lot, was successively an army officer, a banker, and a clergyman, while Francis and Charles, the two youngest, went at twelve into the naval academy and rose to the rank of admiral.

There were also two girls, Cassandra the fifth child, and Jane the seventh. As soon as the younger one could stagger about on her own two little feet she followed Cassandra about like a puppy, and as long as they both lived they were never separated except when visiting. Even then they wrote almost daily.

Today Cassandra is seen as a shadowy figure, revealed, like the moon, only in Jane's reflected light. None of her letters survive, but it is clear that the two natures complemented each other, Jane impulsive and warm, Cassandra steady and prudent. A relative once said: "Cassandra had the merit of a temper under command, but Jane had the happiness of a temper that needed no command." However, they were alike in that both were loved by almost all who knew them.

Mr. Austen chose to educate the boys at home along with his day students, but he sent Cassandra away to school at nine. Jane was in fact too young to go, but her mother said, "If Cassandra were ordered to have her head cut off Jane would insist on losing hers too," so along she went.

While the first school was not a success, for Jane nearly died of diphtheria, the second was delightful. Run by a happy-go-lucky old lady with a cork leg and high-born connections in London and Paris, it occupied a twelfth-century abbey with a large and romantic garden. There the day consisted chiefly of recess, which won the girls' hearts and made the establishment so popular it moved on to London and later to Paris. Jane was nine when she and Cassandra left it. That was all the formal schooling she ever had.

Still, her education went on apace, for Mr. Austen's library contained hundreds of books and she charged right through them without stopping. In this cultivated home only the best of English was spoken, so she grew up with that tool already sharpened, and though she once remarked, "I think I may boast myself to be, with all possible vanity, the most un-learned and uninformed female who ever dared to be an authoress," that was only her modest way. It was the family's custom to gather around the hearth while the rector read aloud some good book, and so active a mind as Jane's could not possibly have escaped a lively education.

Steeped not only in her father's collection of the classics but in the blood-and-thunder romances of the day as well, the young mind began its inventions early. The first sample of her writing appeared in the registry of her father's church where the marriages were recorded. Long afterwards a form was found on which a little girl of eight had written, "A marriage has been planned between Henry Frederick How-ard Fitzwilliam of London and Jane Austen of Steventon." A second marriage, this time between "Edmund Arthur William Mortimer of London and Jane Austen of Steventon" also appeared imminent. Underneath that came a terse announcement of the wedding of "Jack Smith and Jane Smith, late Austen." What tale she was acting out will never be known, but her precocious comic sense can be seen at play in the luxuriant names of Fitzwilliam and Mortimer and the anticlimactic Mr. Smith.

The literature popular in those days was the Gothic romance. Horror was the keynote of these tales of ruined castles infested with ghosts, of captive maids screaming and fainting on the smallest provocation, and one needed a strong stomach to enjoy the worm-eaten corpses one met in an average evening's reading.

The Austen household possessed the necessary stomach, but by the age of fifteen Jane had had her fill of the whole lurid Gothic school and wrote a hilarious satire on it. In one chapter the two heroines, Sophia and Laura, separated from their husbands, suddenly came upon them weltering in their own blood. Jane wrote, "Sophia shrieked and fainted on the ground, while Laura screamed and ran mad, both continuing in this unfortunate situation for an hour and a quarter," after which they were restored by a groan from one of the husbands. He spoke once and instantly expired. "Again Sophia sank into a swoon and Laura raved madly for two hours, and should not then have left off, as she was not in the least fatigued," but Sophia recovered and led her to a cottage, where a variety of further adventures awaited them.

During the years when all the family was at home they often put on charades and theatricals in the sitting room or barn. Jane was still too young to act in the dramas, but her comic sense was useful in composing the charades. The star of these family theatricals was a young cousin, Eliza Hancock, who had been born in India, and had attended fashionable schools in England and France. She added a chic continental tone to the charades, and later was to marry Henry. Before that, however, she would marry a young French count, be widowed by the guillotine and come back to England with her baby son. There are traces of her in some of Jane's works.

Being the youngest of the children, Jane lived for years in an atmosphere of pairing off. James married Ann Mathews and, when she died, Mary Lloyd, the granddaughter of a duke. Edward, after making the Grand Tour of Europe, took

Elizabeth Bridges, the lovely daughter of a baronet, who at once began fifteen straight years of childbearing. Henry, after a considerable wait, married Eliza the glamorous countess.

Cassandra, the beauty of the family, fell in love with a young clergyman who, unfortunately having no private means, was unable to marry. A wealthy kinsman offered him the post of army chaplain and though the climate was murderous in the Caribbean, he and Cassandra estimated that one year's salary would put them on their feet financially. So he sailed for the West Indies and she retired from society and started to prepare her trousseau.

The two youngest boys were by now away at the naval academy, and thus the group at the rectory was thinning out. This provided opportunity for the visits back and forth which brought Jane into contact with so many amusing characters. She did not draw them literally in her books, but she certainly drew from them.

In this prosperous community balls were often held in the great houses, where the minuet was giving place to hornpipes, cotillions, and the French *contredanse*, whose intricate steps required special agility. Jane, who never missed a dance, was noted for the delicacy of her footwork, and though she laughed when people called her a charmer and always insisted she was nothing beside the ravishing Cassandra, the records give a different impression. Tall and very slender, with dancing hazel eyes, curly brown hair and cheeks round and pink, she exuded good humor and a zest for life.

She was unquestionably pretty, and any girl who is pretty and merry is likely to have suitors. Jane had her quota. There was the neighbor Tom Lefroy of Ashe, whom she described as "a very gentlemanly good-looking pleasant young man. He has but one fault—being a great admirer of Tom Jones in Mr. Fielding's new novel, he wears the same colored clothes and his morning coat is a great deal too light." His law career took Tom away to Ireland where in time he became the Right Honorable Chief Justice, but fifty years later he confessed he had once been in love with Miss Jane.

There was also a Mr. Blackall of London, who came to Steventon to visit friends and appeared quite taken with her. Later he told friends he had serious intentions and they warned her that she might expect an offer. She could not have taken him very seriously, for she called him "a piece of noisy perfection," but like any twenty-three-year-old she was set up by the prospect of a proposal. When he failed to appear for the Christmas holidays, she laughed. "I am very well satisfied." Still she must have been a little piqued, for fifteen years later, hearing he had married a young lady, she said, "I should like to know what sort of woman she is. I would wish her to be of a silent turn and rather ignorant, fond of cold veal pies, green tea in the afternoon and a green window-blind at night." Jane was human after all.

While the life of balls, tea parties and drives occupied her in the parlors, another life was going on in the second-floor room she shared with Cassandra. There she had a bookcase and a little box desk, and while Cassandra painted, her youthful scribbling graduated from nonsense to pure art. She would interrupt her writing to read a passage aloud to Cassandra and they would roar over it together. She was embarked on a story about two girls named Elinor and Marianne, in which there was much amusing stuff. But she was not easily pleased with her own writing, and when it was finished she put it aside.

Something else which she did like was buzzing in her head like an imprisoned fly. Out it had to come, and in October, 1796, before she was yet twenty-one, she began a story about a snobbish young man named Darcy and a stubborn girl, Elizabeth Bennet. Cassandra and her parents heard *First Impressions* chapter by chapter. When, after ten months, it was all finished, the neat manuscript was passed around from the house of one brother and aunt and cousin to the next. All were bound to secrecy, for not a soul outside must know that the rector's daughter had daringly written a novel; privately they were nothing if not proud of her accomplishment.

Indeed, they could not get enough of it. Francis' wife begged Cassandra to get the manuscript for her to read once more, but Jane wrote Cassandra: "I shall not let Martha read *First Impressions* again upon any account. She is very cunning, but I see through her design: she means to publish it from memory, and one more perusal would enable her to do it!"

The rector was as proud of her as the rest were and thought the story quite good enough to be published—anonymously, of course. With childlike innocence he wrote Messrs. Cadell of London, Book Publishers, saying that he had in his possession the manuscript of a novel in three volumes. He was not sure, he said, whether it was the custom for publishers to be paid for bringing out books or the other way around, but he would be obliged if Messrs. Cadell would inform him whether they chose to be concerned with the manuscript. The Messrs. Cadell managed to restrain their enthusiasm and refused to have even a look.

Jane took the refusal in stride. Nothing depended on its publication; she had had the fun of writing it, and probably the story would be improved by being put aside for a while. Meanwhile, that earlier story was still buzzing in her head, the one about the two girls, Elinor and Marianne. It still had interesting people in it but they needed to be handled better, so she got it out and began afresh, calling it this time *Sense and Sensibility*.

One of Jane's notable characteristics was her ability to exist on more than one level at once. Twice personal tragedy shook her to the depths without affecting her writing at all, and though for years the thunder of the French Revolution rumbled across Steventon's placid sky, her books, true to life as they are, remained firmly above the holocaust.

About this time the first tragedy occurred. Young Thomas Fowle, Cassandra's fiancé, serving his term in the West Indies, caught yellow fever and died. Though less than twenty-six, Cassandra went into black and donned the widow's cap that signified youth was over.

The two sisters, sharing every thought and emotion, suffered most deeply this anguish. Cassandra later destroyed all references to it, but from their nephew's memoirs written fifty years later one senses her silent fortitude and Jane's enfolding care. One sister must have suffered scarcely less than the other.

Yet it was during this very time that Jane was merrily working out the fortunes of Elinor and Marianne Dashwood. Then, having finished this story, she put it away to begin *Northanger Abbey*. When that was finished she put it away, too. The Messrs. Cadell had not appeared interested in *First Impressions*, so why bother trying them with these new efforts?

The year was 1800. Jane was now twenty-five, full of high spirits, enjoying her popularity at parties and laughing unconcernedly when partners did not appear. With so many married brothers, there were many houses for the sisters to visit, and one or the other was almost always away. Henry and his wife Eliza were being very gay in London, and from there Jane wrote home: "In this scene of dissipation and vice I begin already to feel my morals corrupted." Cassandra, still shrinking from public entertainments, spent most of her time at Godmersham with Edward and his family. She regarded herself as permanently on the shelf, but loyal Jane would not have it so and kept nudging her to get out. "Pray do not forget to go to the Canterbury Ball, I shall despise you most insufferably if you do," she wrote sternly.

The two sailor brothers were doing well at sea, and when

news of Frank's promotion to admiral arrived Jane dashed it off to Cassandra, adding: "There! I may now finish my letter and go and hang myself, for I am sure I can write nothing that will not appear insipid after this."

The only Austen not quite content with things as they were was the eldest son, James, who was slated to succeed his father at the rectory. The hale old gentleman showed no sign of retiring, however, and it seemed that life at Steventon would continue indefinitely in this same relaxed routine. Then one day when Jane and her friend Martha Lloyd were returning from a drive, their world turned turtle. They were met at the door by Mrs. Austen. "Well, girls," she cried, clapping her hands, "it's all settled. Your father has decided to retire and go to live in Bath."

It was the end of a way of life. Jane celebrated it by fainting dead away on the doorstep.

Every gardener knows what happens when a flower is uprooted and transplanted. Sometimes the shock kills it; often its foliage withers; always its growth stops for a while. Jane, suddenly stuck down in a strange spot after twenty-five tranquil years, did not exactly wither, but it was years before the creative sap flowed again.

Meanwhile she made the best of the inevitable. "There is something interesting in the bustle of going away, and the prospect of spending summers by the sea or in Wales is very delightful," she wrote. Besides, Bath was one of the most charming towns in England, with exquisite buildings and a richness of plays, concerts and balls unique outside London. There the Austens found a house with cook, maid and manservant quite close to that of Leigh Perrot and his wife, and as this brother of Mrs. Austen was her one really rich relative, and since the retired Mr. Austen had now but £ 600 a year, they clung hopefully to the connection.

So the parents, the two daughters, and eventually Martha Lloyd as a sort of permanent guest, passed several years in

Bath society, comfortable but never quite rooted there. As Mrs. Austen had become an invalid, either Jane or Cassandra ran the house. But sometimes, with Martha Lloyd substituting for them, the two went off on long leisurely trips among the downs and villages of Devonshire. And here occurred the other shattering event.

There is not even the name of the man involved in it, and no one would ever have known of its occurrence had not Cassandra, many years later, suddenly broken her reserve and confided in her niece. Even so, she gave no details, only relating a story that suggested a peaceful lake thrashed by a sudden storm and then left as smooth and calm as before. But the storm had stirred new depths, and perhaps its tragic sequel contributed to that long period when Jane did little writing. For Jane the merry, Jane the mocking, fell in love.

He was a clergyman, young and very handsome—"One of the most charming persons," Cassandra told her niece, "I ever knew. You know how difficult I should be to please, where my darling was concerned, but I judged him entirely worthy of her." He was visiting his brother, a young doctor, in the neighborhood, and had a room in the same inn where Jane and Cassandra were staying. There they met, and in a few summer days these two found what they had hoped for.

Travel arrangements had been made and the sisters had to move on, but the young man would not say good-bye. "I must see you again," he said. "May I join you later in your tour?"

"Yes," said Jane, and Cassandra knew she was answering more than this one request. A town and a date were named.

The story ended strangely like Cassandra's. When they arrived at the appointed place they were met, not by this young man but by a letter. In a manner and from a cause unknown, he had died.

In Jane's world no well-bred woman hung her woes on the line to be gaped at, and if she wept she hid even the betraying handkerchief. There is no evidence in her novels of her heartbreak; only at the end of *Persuasion,* her last book, which was published after her death, is there perhaps a reference to herself. In it the heroine, discussing the question whether women love more deeply than men, says, "All the privilege I claim for my own sex (it is not an enviable one, you need not covet it) is that of loving longest when hope is gone."

In the meantime she had her life to live and she continued to do so with spirit. "It is no creed of mine," she told her niece once, "that such disappointments kill anybody."

She would not pine away for love, like a Gothic heroine. Neither would she take the "practical" way—not, that is, for long. In 1802 a gentlewoman's life had but one goal, marriage. Failing that, she could be a poor relation in someone else's home or a governess. Jane knew that when her father died she and Cassandra would face that choice; hence her short-lived attempt to avoid it.

She and her sister were staying with James at Steventon when old friends in a nearby town, Catherine and Alethea Bigg, and their brother Harrison, begged them to come for a visit at Manydown Park. All three of them adored Jane, and during the first evening the girls managed to set the stage for their brother's proposal in the conservatory.

Attractive and intelligent, Harrison was heir to Manydown Park and another estate, and it is easy to imagine the arguments flashing through Jane's mind, the comfort, the established position, and best of all the sure home for Cassandra. She accepted him.

When she went up to bed and thought on what she had done, panic shook her. She trembled, her teeth chattered; finally she rushed to Cassandra's room. "We must go, we must leave at once!" she cried, and disregarding her friends' feelings and convenience she insisted on escaping at once. Harrison's weeping sisters drove the girls back to the rectory, but even that was not far enough away and James was forced to take them all the way to Bath. Thus ended Jane's stab at being practical.

This happened during the year after her short-lived love affair. Perhaps she had hoped to fill the emptiness. Or perhaps she was weary of other people's houses and wished for a home of her own. But the price was too high. "Nothing can be compared," she said, "to the misery of being bound without love."

Before leaving Steventon, Jane had written a draft of *Northanger Abbey*, but in the ensuing turmoil it had gone undeveloped. The following year she finished it and sold it to a publisher. But such a sale!—£ 10 and a promise to bring out the manuscript "sometime." The next eight years, however, saw another unproductive period, for the family moved several times, and with Cassandra constantly away at Edward's everything domestic fell to Jane. "I find composition impossible with my head full of mutton and doses of rhubarb," she observed ruefully.

Cassandra's long absences did however stimulate one kind of composition, the chatty letters full of sparkling gossip that tell almost everything that is known of Jane's life. It is tantalizing to think how much more there would be had not Cassandra, in an excess of protectiveness toward Jane, destroyed everything personal and intimate.

In 1805 Mr. Austen died, leaving his wife and daughters only £ 150 a year, so that now the three gentlewomen were indeed poor. Frank took care of them for a year or two; then, thanks to Edward, they came to rest in a home of their own.

Edward's wife had died after the birth of their eleventh child and he, lonely and helpless, brought his womenfolk to live in a pretty cottage on the Chawton estate. Jane was delighted with its gardens and view of the village main street. "You cannot imagine, it is not in human nature to

43

imagine, what a nice walk we have round the orchard," she exulted. "I hear that an apricot has been detected on one of the trees." The house had a parlor, a music room, and six bedrooms, plenty of room for the twenty-five nephews and nieces who loved to visit, assured of entertaining stories and overflowing affection. Anna, the daughter of James, and Edward's eldest, Fanny, were Jane's special favorites and grew with the years into her special friends.

Jane was now over thirty, and like Cassandra she had started wearing a widow's cap. At dances she sat in the music room indulgently watching the young people, and merely laughed when friends tried to marry her off. About one relative's fumbling attempts she wrote Cassandra: "I am much obliged to Mrs. Knight for the interest she takes in me, and she may depend upon it that I *will* marry Mr. Papillon, whatever may be his reluctance or my own."

Unperturbed by her spinsterhood, she kept herself amused in the parlor with a squeaking door. There was no satisfactory desk there, and the family was always coming in and out, but this did not disturb Jane as she scribbled away on the box desk on her lap. She only asked that the squeaking hinge be left unoiled, for it warned of approaching strangers and gave her time to slide the paper she was writing on under the blotter.

For Jane was back at work. Much has been made of the eight years during which she published nothing—too much, actually, for they were not as inactive as they seemed. She made a timid effort to get *Northanger Abbey* published and, as "Mrs. Ashton Dennis," wrote the firm, threatening mildly to take it elsewhere. A sharp reply from the publishers in legal language sent "Mrs. Dennis" scurrying for cover, and Jane never did see the book in print. She also wrote two fragments, "The Watsons," and "Lady Susan." The truth is that the constant moving had disturbed her, and it was only after she was settled into Chawton Cottage that she could relax and think of working again.

There was that story she had been working on so long ago, *Sense and Sensibility*—she loved the characters and thought some of the scenes quite amusing. Perhaps if she worked that one over . . .

Henry, in London, assumed the task of finding a publisher for *Sense and Sensibility*. Mr. Thomas Egerton of the Military Library was sufficiently interested to bring it out though not enough to risk his own money. The anonymous authoress agreed to make good any loss and the story was published. In 1811, few novels were reviewed in literary journals, and Jane, a beginner, had none of the later writer's aids to guide her—no courses in English or journalism, no agent or editor, not even the shoptalk of other writers; she was taught solely by her own instinct. Yet she proved herself at once a true novelist. Her material was the world she knew and the people in it, but she was no mere verbal photographer. "I am too proud of the men in my books," she replied to one inquiry, "to admit that they are only Mr. A. or Colonel B."

Sense and Sensibility, "by a Lady," was a moderate success and brought her £ 140, but its main achievement was to interest the public in the anonymous author and to encourage her to go on writing. Personal fame was to her no consideration, but she did enjoy the activity and the "pewter," so she disinterred the other buried novel, rewrote it, and sent it on to Mr. Egerton. This time he paid her £ 110 outright, and in secret excitement she waited for the debut of her "darling child."

Pride and Prejudice, A Novel in Three Volumes, by the Author of *Sense and Sensibility*, was like a spring dawn, fresh and sunny, with every blade of grass sparkling with dew. Jane herself loved the book and could not resist trying it on a stranger. When the volumes arrived from London, she and her mother invited a Miss Benn for lunch; they had received a new novel by some anonymous author, they said, and would she care to hear it read aloud? Miss Benn was willing, and while Jane watched the guest's face sidelong, Mrs.

Austen began: "It is a truth universally acknowledged, that a single man in possession of a good fortune must be in need of a wife,"—the famous first-chapter introduction of Mr. Bennet, one of the most amusing men in English literature.

Mrs. Austen read well enough, Jane reported to Cassandra, but rather too rapidly. "Nevertheless, Miss Benn really does seem to admire Elizabeth." And, one sister to another, "I must confess that *I* think her as delightful a creature as ever appeared in print, and how I shall be able to tolerate those who think otherwise, I do not know!" But Miss Benn was a very satisfactory guinea pig and wanted to hear more the next morning. And so it has been ever since with readers of *Pride and Prejudice*.

Jane had struck her stride, and in less than two years *Mansfield Park* came out. Here she tried a change of pace, introducing characters less sunny than those of the Bennet circle. But writing about guilt and misery bored Jane; she preferred the part in the novel about the private theatricals— in itself a rare autobiographical note derived from those early melodramas in the Steventon barn.

As one book was being gotten out of the way the next was coming on. But *Emma* had a rough road, for Jane was interrupted by a call to London from the brilliant, mercurial Henry. His wife Eliza had recently died and now he had to be nursed through a long and nerve-racking illness. In the end it was Jane who suffered the most from it, for the strain and anxiety undermined her health.

Henry's illness had a secondary effect: the Prince Regent, acting King during George III's insanity, was a scoundrel and a rake, but he was an art connoisseur as well, and when he heard through Henry's doctor that the author of *Pride and Prejudice* was in London he invited her to visit the royal library. Further, he hinted, he might permit her to dedicate her next novel to him; and though Jane was accustomed to highborn personages, such a privilege could not be ignored. She accepted both invitations.

In spite of this creeping notoriety, she insisted on remaining anonymous, partly from shyness, and partly because she thought fame would distort her normal relationships. Still, she frankly relished praise, and lacking such latter-day pleasures as press clippings, she collected the comments of friends, once wryly recording that "Mrs. Augusta B. thought *S and S* and *P and P* downright nonsense, but expected to like *M P* better, and having finished the first volume flattered herself that she had got through the worst."

Emma came off well with her friends, and brother Charles wrote, "I am delighted with *Emma*, more so, I think, than even with my favorite *P and P*, and have read it three times." It is nice to think that *Emma's* reception was a warm one, for this was the last time Jane was to collect any comments at all.

For four years she had been working very hard—three novels out and another going onto paper. But *Persuasion* was dragging, for her health had begun to falter and her rosy color to fade. Family problems also took their toll: Edward was threatened, through a legality, with the loss of much of his wealth, and to a father of eleven this could be disaster. Even more disturbing, Henry's bank had failed, taking all his goods and much of his family's, including her own £ 13 profit from *Mansfield Park*. Being Henry, however, he bounced cheerfully back into the church and lived out his life as a highly regarded clergyman.

Jane's resilience was not so great—except in her writing, which continued as sharp and clean as ever. It had become perhaps even tenderer, for *Persuasion* seems to recall the lost love of her youth. But she was rapidly slipping away. At times she was strong enough to work, and having bought back the manuscript of *Northanger Abbey* she wrote a Preface for it. That was all she could manage. Treatment by an apothecary at nearby Winchester was recommended, and she was carried, "a very genteel, portable sort of invalid," to furnished rooms there. But it was of no avail, and the gay fragile spirit slipped away in Cassandra's arms on the eighteenth of July, 1817.

Cassandra, who had lived for her sister, went on living for their mother. She had been selfless always, and now in the long empty days she thought she was doing her best. Much as she had valued her sister, she never realized that Jane was no longer hers alone, or that her letters and other papers, which she destroyed with such a merciless hand, now belonged to the world.

Henry, too, was tragically reticent in his stiff little biographical note accompanying the posthumously published *Persuasion* and *Northanger Abbey*. It was only many years later that the family privacy was broken by an elderly nephew in his personal *Memoir of Jane Austen*. And even he would have marveled at the respect accorded these unpretentious stories which Jane had called "little bits of ivory (two inches wide) on which I work with so fine a brush."

"A milestone in English literature," authorities had begun calling these bits of ivory. "A turning point leading to the eventual development of the English novel of character." How amused Jane would have been at the pomposity of it— but how secretly pleased, as well!

Nathaniel Hawthorne
(1804=1864)

Nathaniel Hawthorne

(1804-1864)

"**N**ATHANIEL HAWTHORNE is the handsomest Yankee that ever walked the planet!" So exclaimed the English novelist Trollope, and indeed he may have been, with his rich dark hair and eye "like a violet with a soul in it." He may also have been the most modest, for he described himself quite erroneously as a "mild, shy, gentle, melancholic, exceedingly sensitive and not very forcible man."

The actual truth is somewhat hard to come by, for Nathaniel Hawthorne was two men, one watching and making mock of the other. The author of *The Scarlet Letter* abode in a world of dark crimes and devils in human form, of supernatural visitations and monstrous villainy. Yet he was also a man "marvelously moved to fun." The two sides together emitted a brilliant but chilly luminosity.

Hawthorne was peculiarly the product of his time and place. In 1804 Salem, Massachusetts, had not entirely emerged from its haunted past, for though witches no longer might be burned, books certainly were. There was a grim air to this New England town built by rugged sea captains, and its customhouse, through which passed its rich cargoes, was the scene of Hawthorne's personal crucifixion.

While by 1804 the Hawthorne family had ceased to be affluent, it was one of Salem's oldest. The first Hawthorne had come from England nearly two hundred years before, a harsh magistrate and soldier who showed Quakers no mercy, and his son was one of the notorious judges who presided at the witches' trials in 1692. One of these women had screamed a curse on him as she was dragged to the gallows, and later Nathaniel, with a shiver, accepted it as the cause of the family's decline. He was, he believed, somehow involved in his ancestor's guilt; he dwelt with it constantly, unable to break free, and this burden of sin, this need to be shriven, motivated his literature if not his life.

The father of Nathaniel was a sea captain who had died of fever in South America when his son was only four. There were two daughters also, Elizabeth and Louisa, and after his death the widow and her children moved in with her own family, the Mannings. There the ministrations of eight Manning aunts and uncles, all unmarried, made it inevitable that the beautiful, spoiled little boy should become a somewhat demanding man, but fortunately he was so charming that his servitors—mother, aunts, sisters, wife, and daughters— always felt themselves amply rewarded. Late in life his mother, failing in health, was to withdraw into a seclusion that bred rumors of cloistered Hindu silences, but in Nathaniel's childhood she made a happy home of their carpetless, curtainless rooms.

Nathaniel started to school late, but at six he was already familiar with the classics: *Pilgrim's Progress,* Shakespeare, and Spenser's *Faery Queen* (his first daughter was named Una after the Spenser heroine). At nine a foot injury which put him on crutches for three years gave him even more chance for reading. And then, when his mother moved to Raymond, Maine, his happiest times began, years of fishing, wandering the woods, reading. Here he developed his lifelong taste for solitude. And here he made a lifelong friend, the illegitimate son of a Negro woman and a white lawyer, whom he defended from the taunts of his friends. His sympathy for this boy William Symmes, and for another like him

NATHANIEL HAWTHORNE AT 36
(from portrait by Charles Osgood)

whom he met in college, colored his later treatment of the illegitimate little Pearl in *The Scarlet Letter.*

In 1819, restored in health, he went back to Salem for schooling. His Uncle Robert had agreed to foot the bills, but Nathaniel, who never had a good word for education, protested humorously, "I am sorry you intend to send me to school again. Mother says she can hardly spare me!" Back he went anyway, but to a cheaper one this time. Of this humiliating circumstance he wrote Louisa with a Biblical flourish: "I now go to a five-dollar school, I that have been to a ten-dollar one. Oh Lucifer, son of the morning, how art thou fallen!"

By sixteen he was ready to face the world. He had already written his mother: "I do not want to be a doctor and live by men's diseases, nor a minister and live by their sins, nor a lawyer and live by their quarrels. What do you think of my becoming an author?" An author required an education, however, so to college he went.

Bowdoin College was close to home and, more to the point, cheap: tuition, $8 a term, rent $6.65 a quarter-term, food $2 a week, sweeping and bedmaking, $1. His four college years were undistinguished; he received average marks and the standard fines for cutting class, refusing to declaim in public, playing cards, and visiting the town tavern. But his looks set him apart—slender figure, unusual walk with magnificent head quizzically a little to one side. In manner he was quiet and courteous but so withdrawn that one of his best friends said: "I love Hawthorne. I admire him. But I do not know him. He lives in a mysterious world of imagination which he never permits me to enter." Nevertheless, friendships he made at Bowdoin with Franklin Pierce (later to become President), Horatio Bridge, and Henry Wadsworth Longfellow figured at the crucial moments of his life.

Young intellectuals of the day were becoming impatient with the national preference for British authors, and Longfellow in his commencement oration proclaimed: "Palms are to be won by native writers. Of the many causes which have retarded the growth of literature in our country, the greatest is the want of *attention!*"

Hawthorne, who stated modestly, "I know I shall never make a distinguished figure in the world," nevertheless shared the ferment. In college he wrote several tales and part of a novel. After graduation in 1825 he went back to Salem and, living on his father's small legacy, began twelve years of almost complete solitude.

Some describe this hermit period as a neurotic withdrawal from life; others see it merely as deep concentration on his art. At all events, for all these years he lived alone in a room in his mother's house without speaking to a soul outside his family for months together. At twilight he left his "dismal chamber" to walk along the beach, and once a year took a two-week vacation. Otherwise, as he said later, "I sat by the wayside of life like a man under enchantment, with a thick shrubbery springing up around me until no exit appeared possible through the entangling obscurity." This does sound neurotic, and the years were certainly barren of physical action. But another kind of action was raging within, the unseen gestation from which was to come rich fruit.

During this time he finished the novel he had begun in college, and with some of the $1,400 he had inherited from his father, he published it anonymously. But no sooner did he see the amateurish effort, entitled *Fanshawe*, in print than he destroyed his copies in a storm of disgust. Today any copy of the original edition is a prized collector's item.

In college he had tried another field more to his taste, short stories, and now he finished seven of them. Seventeen booksellers, however, turned him down at once, for no publisher would gamble on an unknown American writer when they could reissue, without having to pay royalties, the most successful English books. Finally, in despair, he turned on his manuscripts with loathing. "I feel a physical sickness whenever I glance at them," he cried. "I shall take a wild enjoyment in seeing them in the blaze." This was the same sober young man whose wildest dissipation was taking a cup of chocolate with his sisters in the late afternoon.

Then, after four years he sold a story. Despite his discouragement he had been unable to stop writing, and, at last, a man named Goodrich gave him $35 for a tale and published it anonymously. It opened the door a crack, but still his sales were always made under the same mean conditions, for Goodrich saw a gold mine in this humble writer and crammed his annual story collection, *The Token*, with Nathaniel's work. "As they are anonymous there is no objection to having so many pages by the same author," the man said candidly, and forty-four tales and sketches had appeared before a soul knew the author's name. Thus, unknown and unreviewed, Hawthorne earned less than $300 a year.

These years of frustration left him with what Goodrich described as a "sarcastic mouth and aspect cold, moody and distrustful." They left him also with a nightmare which kept recurring into old age: that he was still at college, still struggling and unknown, while his contemporaries had long since moved on to eminence.

The only easement he could afford was the annual outing in New England, and even here nothing diverting happened; he merely observed and chatted, recording incidents and personalities in a notebook. He did meet several attractive girls—a fisherman's freckled daughter in Massachusetts, a landlady's daughter in Maine, a tall dark-eyed queenly maid on Martha's Vineyard, but his pursuit was timid and brief and they only supplied him with models for later heroines.

At last, disturbed by the tone of desolation in his letters, his college friend Horatio Bridge wrote: "There is a kind of desperate coolness that seems dangerous. I fear that you are too good a subject for suicide." Bridge admonished him briskly, "I have been trying to think why you are so miserable. Although you have not much property, you have good health and powers of writing. I wish to God I could impart to you a little of my own brass."

This kind friend went beyond simply giving advice; he quietly offered Goodrich $250 to bring out a collection of stories on condition that the author's name appear on them. So, at last, with *Twice-Told Tales,* Nathaniel Hawthorne emerged from that entangling obscurity and "opened an intercourse with the world."

At this point another college friend, Henry W. Longfellow, who by now had considerable prestige as a writer for the *North American Review,* gave him an ecstatic review. Hawthorne wrote him gratefully: "Whether or no the public will agree with your praise, there are at least five persons who think you the most sagacious critic on earth, viz., my mother, and two sisters, my old maiden aunt, and, the sturdiest believer of the five, myself."

Though *Twice-Told Tales* had only a mild success, it was a turning point, for now other publishers knew where to go for powerful, offbeat stories. Further, it consolidated his friendship with Longfellow, led to a political appointment and prosperity, and found him a wife. There is no doubt which of the three he prized the highest.

Dr. Nathaniel Peabody, a dentist of Salem, had three sons and three daughters. The boys made no mark, but the girls were memorable. Elizabeth was the eldest, an intellectual and reformer who made a point of knowing everyone who *did* something. Mary also was an intellectual, and later married Horace Mann, founder of Antioch College. The youngest, Sophia, had suffered devastating headaches since childhood, and now, at twenty-six, spent her time in her room painting and reading English, Latin, Greek and Hebrew. Intense and highly emotional, Sophia had a keen mind, an impulsive temper, and, it must be admitted, not much humor.

Nathaniel Hawthorne

In 1837 Elizabeth, having read *Twice-Told Tales* and learned that she and the Hawthornes had played together as children, invited them to call. When she saw Nathaniel and his sisters coming up the walk, she greeted them breathlessly and then rushed upstairs. "Sophia," she cried, bursting into the invalid's room, "get up, get dressed. The Hawthornes are downstairs, and he's the handsomest creature you ever saw. Like Lord Byron, only even better."

On the theory that invalids should never marry, Sophia had—or thought she had—no interest in men, and she only laughed at Elizabeth's excitement. "I don't want to get dressed. You talk to them."

"But don't you want to see him? He's extravagantly handsome."

"If you're nice to him," Sophia said soothingly, "he'll call again. Then I'll see him." Her guess was correct; he did call, and this time she came down, clothed in a long robe all white and flowing. When Elizabeth said, "Here is my sister Sophia," Nathaniel glanced up, and then looked again sharply and hard. During the afternoon she spoke little, but when she did, in her low, sweet voice, Elizabeth noted his piercing gaze. What, she thought, if he should fall in love with her? It would be tragic, with Sophia so set against marriage.

He called yet again, and this time Sophia came down eagerly, a poetic picture with a single fragant violet in her hand. The visit was short, but afterwards she noted in her diary his brilliant smile and celestial expression. Clearly, her indifference was dwindling.

On subsequent calls they took walks together and sat under the trees, she drawing and he reading aloud. Then he came to announce that he was going away for three months and no one, not even his mother, was to know where.

Wandering through the Berkshires and Green Mountains, he meditated on marriage, analyzing himself, analyzing Sophia. "I am slow to feel," he admitted to his notebook, "slow to comprehend. Like the anaconda I need to lubricate any object a great deal before I can swallow it and actually make it my own." Pondering on Sophia, he recognized that she was not what he would have prescribed for himself. Humorous and skeptical, he shied away from raptures, and Sophia was given to rapturous flights. She was graceful and alive. Still, she was not beautiful. Moreover, she was a shade too intellectual. Some of the ladies in the Peabody circle, notably Margaret Fuller with her high-flown talk about women's rights, were rather hard to take.

Nevertheless, when he returned, there were more walks together, and by the end of the year Sophia's admiration—indeed, by this time her passionate adoration—overbalanced all else. They became engaged, but since Hawthorne was nervous about his own womenfolk's reaction they kept their plans dark.

With marriage looming, he needed to be practical, and here his college friends Bridge and Franklin Pierce, who knew a number of politicians, and Elizabeth Peabody, who knew everybody, came in handy. Hawthorne was made measurer of coal and salt in the Boston Custom House at $1,500 a year. Not princely, but a living.

Thrust suddenly into the world, he found he enjoyed grubbing about in the holds of grimy ships among Arabs and Icelanders, relished the brawls and racy talk of the lowly and unwashed. But eventually the heat and cold and heavy labor wore down his enthusiasm and after two years he resigned.

Meanwhile Elizabeth had been brewing yeasty plans. The Peabody family had moved to Boston and founded a bookstore. There Ralph Waldo Emerson, Bronson Alcott, Henry Thoreau, Margaret Fuller, and the other Transcendentalists gathered to discuss Brook Farm, the Utopian community where all were to share plain living and high thinking. Elizabeth, a prime mover, dragged Sophia along, and for her sake Hawthorne subscribed $1,000 and joined as a farmhand.

But in spite of the Peabody earnestness he could not swallow Brook Farm. Reform, he felt, must be spontaneous, from the heart, and professional reformers were too often crackpots. In the meantime, his $1,000 was gone and after eight months he was no nearer marriage than before.

During the separation the lovers' letters accumulated. Hers have not survived, for he destroyed them jealously, but his, often employing the passionate and reverent "Thou," she treasured. "Thou hast taught me that I have a heart," he wrote. "It is a miracle, to have converted a life of shadows into the deepest truth by thy magic touch. God gave thee to me to be the salvation of my soul." He was convinced that their love would restore her health: "I will have faith in its efficacy. Partake of my health and strength, my beloved. Let me be your peace, as you are mine." But humor kept breaking through. "Yet I should be almost afraid of some radical transformation. If you cannot grow plump and rosy and tough and vigorous without being changed into another nature, then I do think, for this short life, you had better remain as you are."

As the years passed, one, two, three, four, their unfulfilled passion became unbearable. His other employments had convinced him he must sink or swim by his writing; and having persuaded a magazine to take a certain number of his stories yearly, he decided that at thirty-eight he had waited long enough. He told his womenfolk of his plans to marry, and though they were frigid with shock at first, he persuaded them to accept the idea.

The wedding was set for the first of July, 1842, but Sophia had one last nervous relapse. Finally, however, on July 9th, their sublime union began. "Now," cried Hawthorne, "I feel as if for the first time in my life, I was awake. I have found reality."

They started a diary together, and Sophia poured her joy into it: "Oh lovely God, how I exult in his love! I am Spring with all its birds, its rivers, its buds—singing, rushing, blooming in his arms. I feel new as the earth which is just born again. I rejoice that I am, because I am his—wholly, unreservedly his. Therefore is my life beautiful and gracious. Therefore is the world pleasant as roses." The marvel is that such ecstasy was to last for their full lifetime together and, for her, even after his death. Marvelous too was its effect on her health. Like Elizabeth Barrett Browning, she rose bodily off her sickbed into a wiry resilience that amazed her family and, in her sightseeing days abroad, exhausted the sturdiest of them.

Life in their old Concord house was blissful, she moving about in hushed reverence while he wrote furiously upstairs, seventeen stories and a potboiler for his good friend Bridge. Nathaniel's reputation grew apace, with even the caustic critic Edgar Allan Poe declaring, "Mr. Hawthorne's distinctive trait is invention, creation, imagination, originality—a trait which in fiction is worth all the rest." But magazines paid when, and if, they chose, and the Hawthornes were sorely pressed after their daughter Una's birth in 1844.

Again he had to ask his political friends for help toward a steady job, but they were Democrats and as long as the Whigs were in power there was not much they could do. Bridge and Pierce, however, kept trying; their whole circle sought assistance in Washington to save this eminent man from dying of starvation and demanded, for the honor of party and country, that he be given a political appointment. One door after another opened and shut, and it was two years and another baby before President Polk finally made him Surveyor and Custom Inspector for Salem, at $1,200 per annum.

During the years of steady employment that followed, Hawthorne wrote little, for the sense of security they gave him had an enervating effect which was sparked only by his joy in his family. Then, in 1848, a Presidential election threw his party out of power again and opponents came gunning for his job.

Nathaniel Hawthorne

In a scandal that electrified all New England, he was charged with malfeasance in office and withholding, for his own use, some of his employees' salary, and though he denied the charges and fought back bitterly, he was cast out ignominiously. This public crucifixion was a time of horror for Hawthorne and his wife, but their trials served to reveal a Sophia transformed by love. Airy and impractical in easier times, under stress she showed a pair of feet planted firmly on the ground. During Nathaniel's earning days she had been saving part of her household allowance, and now she handed it back with a bright smile, saying, "I'm glad you lost that job. Now you can get back to your book and do the things you were meant for." Cheerfully she painted lampshades to sell to her friends, who, meanwhile, took up a subscription to keep the little family going.

In shamed gratitude Hawthorne flung himself into his work with a ferocity that frightened Sophia, writing nine hours a day to repay their goodness or die trying. But in his nervous state he was unable to withstand the shock of his mother's sudden death and he collapsed in delirium. This illness, quixotically, brought him fame.

The Boston publisher, James T. Fields, hearing of his ill-health and depression, came to see him and found him white and shivering in his upstairs study. To brighten the atmosphere, Fields asked about his work.

Hawthorne shook his head. "I can't write. I'll never write anything good again—even supposing I ever have."

"Nonsense," Fields boomed, "I'll wager that right now you've got something ready for a publisher."

He received a sour smile. "What publisher would want anything from the most unsuccessful writer in America?"

This was Fields' moment. "I would. Sight unseen."

"You're mad."

"I mean it. You must have been working on something. Let me see it."

Hawthorne only shook his head again, so Fields looked at

his watch and rose, sighing. "Well, my train leaves in a few minutes." As he passed a tall chest he found himself unexpectedly saying, "That chest, now. What masterpiece have you got hidden in that chest? Come on, let me see it." Even this challenge had no effect, so he shrugged and started for the stairs. "Well, so be it."

Halfway down there was an excited cry: "Fields! Wait!" and Hawthorne came tumbling after him with a roll of manuscript. "I don't know how you knew it was there, but here it is. It's either very good or very bad, I don't know which." On the train Fields read the first draft of the unfinished novel *The Scarlet Letter*.

Hawthorne was amazed at Fields' excited reaction to the manuscript, but it was the incentive he needed and, suddenly bright-eyed and brisk, he set himself to finish the story. Several months later he mailed it with a humble note: "Perhaps you will not like the book or think well of its prospects, and then of course I shall not consider you under any obligation to publish it."

He need not have worried, for the book pleased nearly everyone. Fields now had an author with whom he was to work profitably for many years, and Hawthorne had sudden fame and the prospect of money—the sales stimulated by the notoriety of the customhouse scandal! Most critics gloried in this newly discovered talent though some were repelled by the book's gloom and "immorality." One London critic neatly straddled the two positions: "If Sin and Sorrow in their most fearful forms are to be represented in a work of art, they have rarely been presented with loftier severity, purity and sympathy than in *The Scarlet Letter*."

Only Salem was aghast. Hawthorne, knowing the book contained neither light nor cheer, had thought to brighten it with a satirical Foreword about his customhouse days, and soon after publication he wrote Bridge: "My preliminary chapter has caused the greatest uproar since witch times. If I escape from town without being tarred and feathered I shall consider it good luck." Thereafter the name of Hawthorne was anathema in Salem for fifty years.

The icy reception drove the Hawthorne family to take refuge in a little red house in the Berkshires, where they were welcomed by a literary colony including James Russell Lowell, Oliver Wendell Holmes and that strange, deep man, Herman Melville.

Although Melville was fifteen years Hawthorne's junior, the two fierce and witty men were natural friends. In reviewing *Mosses from an Old Manse* Melville had noted the other's "deep and noble nature," his "sense of blackness ten times black, derived from his Calvinistic sense of Innate Depravity and Original Sin, from whose visitations no deeply thinking mind is wholly free." It was appropriate that he should dedicate his own profound masterpiece, *Moby Dick,* to this friend.

The two stimulated each other's will to work, with *Moby Dick* and *The House of the Seven Gables* being spun out side by side. Sophia, pregnant with her third child, lay on the couch while Hawthorne read this favorite of all his stories aloud each evening. She discerned in it "unspeakable grace and beauty," and when it was published in 1851 its success surpassed that of *The Scarlet Letter.* There was humor in his writing this time, and some called it the best history of New England ever written.

However, after a year of gradually increasing prosperity, a curious restlessness overtook Hawthorne. "I hate Berkshire with my whole soul," he wrote to a friend. "I detest it! I detest it!! I detest it!!!" After so many exclamation points there had to be a change, and the family went to live in "Hillside," Bronson Alcott's house in Concord. "I have always sat by the wayside of life, like a man under enchantment," Hawthorne had said. So "Hillside" became "Wayside." It was the only place, he said, that ever seemed like home to him, and he was happy there, except during his life's one great tragedy.

His sister Louisa, a favorite of them all, was trapped in a

burning steamboat and, trying to escape, had jumped into the water and drowned. The whole family was grief-stricken, and Hawthorne was badly shaken, but again Sophia showed her inner steel. With an unqualified faith in immortality, she wrote her mother, "It is a positive bliss to me to contemplate Louisa and her mother together again. If there is anything immortal in life it is the home relations. God never has knit my soul to my husband's soul for such a paltry moment as this human life. I have not loved my mother for one short day! My children do not thrill my heartstrings with less than an eternal melody. We know that God cannot trifle." In spite of the ornate language one feels her absolute sincerity; and the real test of it, her own husband's death, when it came, only proved its genuineness.

At this time Franklin Pierce was nominated for the Presidency. In the face of rising antislavery agitation, he stood for states' rights, and Hawthorne, distrusting reforms coming from the law rather than the heart, and calling slavery an evil soluble by God alone, supported him and wrote his campaign biography. This gave him a certain political standing and he found himself flattered and sought after. This was all very pleasant after the bitterness of the Salem days, and for a while the novelist frankly relished the taste of politics. Moreover, he learned after the inauguration that Pierce was looking about for a rich plum for his friend, and he let it be known that he yearned to explore his English roots. It happened that the richest plum available was the Liverpool consulship, so in July, 1853, the family sailed away to the boom of cannon saluting Nathaniel Hawthorne, famous author and Presidential appointee.

Hawthorne's seven years abroad brought him $30,000, and three hundred thousand words in travel notes, some of which were published as *Our Old Home*, but they did not bring him another *Scarlet Letter*. His duties as consul were on the whole depressing, for the destitute and the beggar were his principle charges. He spent his days in morgues, hospitals, undertakers' parlors, law courts, and steamship offices, and personally aided many an injured United States sailor. But as often as possible he got out of Liverpool, taking his family sightseeing—to Uttoxeter, where Dr. Johnson had made a famous confession in the public square that always fascinated Hawthorne; to Manchester, where a great art exhibition had been assembled; to London, where he met the bright, the beautiful, the famous. There he noted that Robert Browning was handsome, simple, agreeable, and that Elizabeth Barrett Browning had a voice so thin and high it was as if a grasshopper were speaking.

But (like that anaconda of old) he could not swallow and digest things all at once, and at first he was shocked by England's extremes of wealth and poverty and her preoccupation with the country's antiquity. Later he changed so much as to call it his spiritual home, and to remark that "The United States are fit for many excellent purposes but they are certainly not fit to live in."

He was of course always pondering his next great book, and thought he had found it in a house five hundred years old. There had long been growing in his mind an idea for a story about an American, such as himself, who had returned to England to claim an ancestral estate, and when he was shown a dark stain on the floor which, according to legend, was the blood of a martyr, he pricked up his ears. The story was suitably Gothic: the man had been committed to prison for his faith and had stamped his foot in protest, whereupon blood had poured from his shoe and no scrubbing had ever been able to wash it away. Hawthorne tried over and over to fit the bloody footstep into a story but was never satisfied with the result.

In truth, all his satisfactions were running thin. Turning against England and that "black and miserable hole of Liverpool," he moved to Italy when his four-year term was up.

Here he hoped to be happy, though living in Italy was Sophia's lifelong dream, not his. There, shedding tears of ecstasy, she sketched numberless statues, palaces, fountains and gardens, and wore out her family with her dogged sight-seeing.

There Hawthorne, as in England, blew hot and cold. One day he could say, "Rome certainly does draw itself into my heart as London or Concord or Salem never did"; and on another, "I hate the Roman atmosphere, it has a kind of malignity." But he kept at his self-education, with especial attention to that peculiar phenomenon, the American artist abroad. Later, in *The Marble Faun*, he made this type so fascinating that it was said he had inadvertently lured American girls to Rome by the shipload.

The Marble Faun was developing without his knowledge. He was possessed by Guido's portrait of Beatrice Cenci and her look of horrified innocence. At the same time, he kept returning to Praxiteles' statue of a faun, that creature half animal, half man, and altogether immune from human emotions. Though he had long been wrestling with the Bloody Footstep, this lighthearted sprite kept intruding on his thoughts, and at last he gave way and started the story ruled by his old obsession, the idea of salvation achieved through the sufferings of sin.

But before *The Marble Faun* was finished, his old restlessness returned. Sick of Italy but dreading America, he stalled for another year in England, but that too palled and at last he had to face the reality of going home. This was even more depressing. His family life was still without flaw and he was one of America's favorite authors, but he was tormented by that blackness ten times black which Melville had detected in him, that sense of Depravity and Original Sin. Little things and big upset him overmuch; he altered "Wayside" expensively to suit his writing whims, then could not write there; visitors irritated him so that he dodged behind trees when they came upon him when he was out walking. Worst of all, the Bloody Footstep absolutely refused to be worked into a book.

His notes on the margins of his manuscripts betray his panic: "The stubborn old devil will not move. . . . There may be a germ in this, I don't know. . . . Now, as for the girls? . . . The life is not yet breathed into this plot, not a spark of passion as yet. Alas, me! How, how, how? . . . All this amounts to just nothing. I don't advance a step. . . . He lives a solitary life, why? A propensity for drink? A tendency to feed on horseflesh? A love of toads? The old bloody footstep business? No, that won't do. . . . Try again. . . . So easily said, so impossible to do. Lackaday!" And so on, agonizingly.

Spring brought the Civil War. He could not believe in it, but it was there, his most gruesome imaginings made manifest. Fiction was nonsense now, but still, with a house and family on his shoulders, he had to write. On and on he worked. *Dr. Grimshaw's Secret. Septimius Felton.* A story about an old man and an elixir of life. Sophia, watching him with desperate anxiety, sensed the dreadful truth.

There seemed to be no disease, but, still not sixty, he was simply shrinking away. Time and again he returned to a childish game he and Una had once played: she had asked him to write the numbers "64" on her hand, as if they had some special meaning, and he had grown into the habit of writing it on paper, "64 . . . 64 . . . 64." When 1863 turned into 1864, everyone noticed how often he wrote the figures.

One day when the subject of immortality had been mentioned, he had said, "Ah, I hope there will be a break . . . a couple of thousand years of sleep before I begin again." He was growing very tired.

Not long afterwards he got the rest he desired. On May 18, 1864, he died in his sleep. He was buried simply, with Emerson, Longfellow, Holmes, Whittier, Lowell, Alcott and many other friends standing by. Some expected Sophia to crumble, but the faith that had kept her joyful after Louisa's death lifted her now, and she cried, "My Father gave me the richest destiny for many years, and I am struck dumb with an ecstasy of gratitude. The darkest cloud has broken into ten thousand singing birds."

Many times—in *The Scarlet Letter, The Marble Faun* and elsewhere—Hawthorne implied a similar vision, a dark cloud transformed into beauty, redemption won through suffering:

> The human heart is a cavern. At the entrance are sunshine and flowers. You step within and find yourself surrounded by monsters and a terrible gloom. It seems like Hell itself. You wander long without hope. But at last a light strikes and you find yourself in a region rich again with the flowers and beauty of the entrance, but this time all perfect. These are the depths of human nature; the gloom and terror may lie deep, but deeper still is the eternal beauty.

Despite his gloom and terror, happily for him, this was his ultimate conviction.

Edgar Allan Poe
(1809=1849)

Edgar Allan Poe
(1809-1849)

THE genius of Edgar Allan Poe was like one of those twisted, undernourished trees one occasionally sees springing from the face of a rocky cliff, whose very survival is against all logic. Poe's environment, his ancestry, most of all his character, were against his ever writing a noteworthy line. Yet with not an inch of favoring soil to root in, this extraordinary plant produced an abundant growth, and it is hardly strange that the fruit tasted of decay and death.

His times, likewise, were against him. American authors were read little and seldom paid, and almost to the end Poe was giving his works away free while borrowing money to feed his family.

His mother, Betty Arnold, had been a child actress who was brought from England in 1796. At nine she was earning her own living; at fifteen she was married and soon afterward became a widow. Later she married a singularly untalented actor named David Poe. This young man had "disgraced" his family by adopting the stage, and managed thereafter to distinguish himself chiefly by a taste for liquor and a distaste for responsibility. David Poe borrowed money for his wedding, and for the duration of his short marriage continued to borrow it, a total failure as an actor and, increasingly, as a husband.

Betty, on the other hand, being gifted and pretty, was

always able to find engagements. This was too much for David's pride, and he drank more and more. Finally he disappeared forever, leaving the twenty-four-year-old girl, with two babies and a third coming, penniless and ill of tuberculosis. David's father took in the older boy, William Henry, but Betty kept Edgar and continued working bravely, with time out for Rosalie's birth, until her death.

This came soon enough, in a dingy lodging house in Richmond, Virginia. Little Edgar's earliest impressions, therefore, were of crushing poverty, illness, and death, things that were to haunt him forever after.

Two kindly young Richmond matrons, Mrs. John Allan and Mrs. William Mackenzie, visited the dying actress and decided to take the children home with them, the baby Rosalie falling to Mrs. Mackenzie when Mrs. Allan made a special plea for the adorable three-year-old boy with the enormous gray eyes.

Here, thought the gentle Frances Allan, might be the answer to her prayers. Her husband, a successful importer and tobacco merchant, longed for a son, and after eight years of marriage she had failed to give him any child at all. Perhaps the lively, precocious little boy might satisfy his wish for fatherhood. (She could not know that in the back streets of Richmond two women—a certain Mrs. Elizabeth Wills and another woman named Collier—had already satisfied that wish. That was Mr. Allan's secret, and it did not come out until much later.)

At the time of Betty Poe's death, John Allan came upon another dark secret. Going through the dead woman's pathetic store of possessions, he found a packet of letters intimating that she had had a lover and that Rosalie was this man's child. Instead of charitably destroying the letters, he carefully stored them away. It is not known how he planned to use them, but certainly they proved a handy weapon against his foster son later on.

EDGAR ALLAN POE
(from the earliest authentic portrait)

Edgar Allan Poe

Despite a cruel hawk nose and small, sharp eyes, John Allan was less deliberately vicious than simply hard-headed and sure of his own righteousness. He was capable, at first, of generosity and love toward the bright, intelligent little boy, reflecting with satisfaction that he was to have an heir after all, a successor to his business and a bearer of his name. He even had him baptized as "Edgar Allan."

And yet . . . and yet . . . there was that unstable theatrical background, the drunken father, the mother of dubious morals. It was one thing to give a child a home and education, but to adopt him legally and assume lifelong responsibility—that was something else. Better, perhaps, to wait a little and see.

Meanwhile, in the handsome house on Fourteenth Street, Edgar enjoyed every luxury. There were the indulgent "Pa" and "Ma" and a houseful of slaves, all bent on coddling him. There was a pleasant school in Richmond, and later a long visit with Allan connections in England and Scotland, and several years in an English school. All Pa's relatives were impressed by the boy's charm and brilliance, and at this point he came close to being formally adopted by his generous foster-father.

Back in Richmond, however, he grew into adolescence and then things changed. He insisted on choosing his own reading—English literary magazines, Byron and other romantic poets. He learned to read Latin and French authors in the original. He composed, at fifteen, a collection of poems addressed with fine impartiality to almost every girl in Miss Mackenzie's elegant Seminary for Young Ladies.

All this was not what the startled merchant had bargained for. When he demanded Edgar's attendance in the office after school, the boy sat behind the counter scribbling verses instead of measuring off imported yard goods, and nothing about business could catch his interest. And on the young poet's announcement that he was going to be a second Lord

Byron, John Allan realized that his hesitation regarding adoption had been well advised.

"A poet, eh?" The small eyes narrowed and the hawk nose jutted aggressively. "And what will you live on? I suppose a poet could buy the luxuries I give you? *Give* you, don't forget, out of charity. Remember that what you don't earn you don't own." Publicly, in front of his friends, the boy was taunted about his penniless orphan state.

Reared by Frances Allan as a Virginia gentleman, Edgar's manners were naturally sunny and winning, but as his pride was attacked his disposition clouded over, and he began picking fights in school and showing off his learning. It was no way to make himself loved, and, alone more and more, the boy with the wide forehead and long-lashed glowing eyes could be seen almost daily in the fields declaiming poetry aloud. The merchant was puzzled and outraged.

It was about this time that Mrs. Allan learned of her husband's illegitimate children, and in her distress she turned to Edgar, then in his early teens, for sympathy. The woman and the boy drew together in an alliance against the man. Mr. Allan had no retaliatory weapon against his virtuous wife, but Edgar was more vulnerable; Allan now brought out that packet of his mother's letters revealing the shameful truth about Rosalie's birth. Each side was thus armed with a lethal weapon—Allan's illegitimate son and daughter against Edgar's illegitimate sister—and the fine house was split down the middle by bitter warfare.

Such a world was too harsh for Edgar Poe. He needed the cushioning of feminine love, and though Mrs. Allan mothered him tenderly, she was not the aerial sprite a young poet needed. At fifteen he found his dream.

While visiting a schoolmate, Bob Stanard, he was introduced to his friend's mother. Only twenty-nine, with an eerie beauty part flesh and part pure light, Mrs. Stanard was to the adolescent like a glimpse of the sun. Over the ensuing months she gave him generous attention, listening gravely to his poems, encouraging, suggesting, best of all, understanding. She inspired while he adored, and both were satisfied. It was perhaps the only time in his life he ever felt at ease.

But disaster always seemed to lie in wait for Edgar Poe. Perhaps he and Mrs. Stanard were so close because they were spirits similarly doomed. At all events, when he came to her house one day, he was told she was ill. He saw her only once more, and by then there was no light in the lovely features. The mind was sinking into darkness, and, mercifully, the body soon went too. Edgar was terrified; death, which had taken his mother, had returned for another, young and fair. His pen gave him his only relief, and the poem "To Helen" was the outpouring of his youthful despair.

But at sixteen one cannot mourn forever, and he buried his pain in love for Elmira Royster, daughter of a friend of the Allans. As John Allan was one of Richmond's wealthiest citizens, the Roysters made no objection when the two sixteen-year-olds spent their afternoons together playing the flute and piano. They were undisturbed even when Edgar wrote poems to Elmira. Thus encouraged, the young couple swore themselves to each other.

College loomed ahead for Edgar. John Allan was losing patience with the bickering over his infidelities, and although Mrs. Allan's declining health promised him an early release, getting rid of the youth was still a problem. The University of Virginia, situated at some distance, seemed to be the answer, so off Edgar went to Charlottesville.

Letters flew back and forth between the young lovers so thickly that the aroused Mr. Royster decided on a frank talk with Mr. Allan. What he learned of the boy's real prospects was a shock, but the problem suggested its own easy remedy —the interception of his daughter's mail. The correspondence abruptly ceased, as Elmira looked in vain for Edgar's letters and he looked in vain for hers. Meantime, her parents pointed out the fickleness of the Poe boy and the charms of another suitor, the rich Mr. Barrett Shelton.

At college Edgar, fretting over Elmira, was having other troubles. On his departure his guardian had given him $110, but he soon learned that he needed $149 for entrance fee at once, and $200 more later. In a panic he wrote to Mr. Allan, who sent him $40. The $149 paid, he then had exactly one dollar left, and again he wrote an appealing letter. This time $100 arrived, but this still left him short $100, with nothing for food and incidentals.

Mr. Allan's intention was to embarrass the youth into either knuckling under or getting out of his household, but he actually achieved a third alternative. Edgar, ashamed to admit he was being deliberately starved, tried gambling, but the cards ran badly and he soon owed $2,000.

Drinking came just as quickly. A natural alcoholic, a single glass of peach-honey wine could set him off on a firework display of talk that fascinated his companions and gave him a temporary sense of superiority. Liquor also blurred his misery over Elmira, over dear Ma's illness, his guardian's heartlessness, his poverty, the secret of his sister's shameful birth. Homesick and bewildered, he cried for help and no help came. "It was then," he wrote Mr. Allan reproachfully, "that I became dissolute . . . because no one cared for me or loved me." This was his eternal cry: Give me money, give me love. Help me or I die.

When he went home at Christmastime a severe blow met him. Elmira was engaged to Barrett Shelton and her door was barred to him. Only later did he learn the truth, and then, in his mind, he and Elmira became Romeo and Juliet, martyrs to their elders' malice.

Still another blow followed when Mr. Allan refused to pay Edgar's gambling debts and ordered him to work out his board and lodging bills. There were arguments and a terrible table-banging scene ending in an ultimatum from Mr. Allan:

no more drinking, no more gambling, no more wasting time writing verse. Buckle down to business or the law. Otherwise, get out. Take twelve hours to think it over.

Edgar could as easily have given up breathing as writing, and on the night of March 18, 1837, his only possible choice was made. Charging out with nothing but the clothes he stood in, he left behind food, security, and Mrs. Allan, the one person who loved him. With his last few dollars he got to Boston and there, pride deflated by hunger, wrote to Allan: "Send me, I entreat you, some money immediately. If you fail to I tremble for the consequences." And later: "I am in the greatest necessity, not having tasted food since yesterday morning." There was no answer, and in desperation he enlisted in the army.

During the next two years there were only two events in his life worth noting: he persuaded a friend to print his long poem *Tamerlane,* not a copy of which was sold (ninety years later he would have gloated to hear $11,600 bid for a single copy) and he spent a number of months at Fort Moultrie, South Carolina. What he heard there of pirate raids and buried treasure served him well in later years for the plot of "The Gold Bug."

Though a surprisingly adequate soldier, he felt trapped in the ranks and once more wrote Allan, begging for help toward a West Point appointment. Mrs. Allan by then was dying and, softened by her pleas in Edgar's behalf, her husband wrote to the authorities in Washington. He also permitted Edgar to come home. But the visit was too late, and for the third time the young man found that death had taken the young and beautiful. It was the theme that seemed to haunt his mind, his life, his work.

Released from the army by paying a substitute to serve his term, a common practice at the time, he waited months for the West Point appointment, and in his impatience once walked from Baltimore to Washington and back in order to make inquiries about it. Meantime, he moved in with relatives, the Clemms.

Edgar's grandmother on the Poe side, paralyzed and senile, lived in Baltimore on a small government pension with her thirty-nine-year-old daughter. This Mrs. Maria Clemm, Edgar's aunt, was a woman of extraordinary courage and loyalty. Besides her mother, she was caring for Edgar's brother Henry, who was dying of tuberculosis, drink and drugs, and for her own worthless son Henry and her small daughter Virginia. Miraculously, she now managed to stretch the monthly $20 pension to include Edgar.

Seven-year-old Virginia, with startlingly violet eyes and waxen skin, came to adore the nineteen-year-old cousin who took time to help her with her lessons every night, and though the house crawled with illness and poverty it was made livable by their laughter and Mrs. Clemm's embracing love.

While waiting for Washington to move on his appointment, Edgar bombarded publishers with his poems, but when no one would buy he was glad to give them away. To the *Yankee and Boston Literary Gazette* he sent "Heaven," accompanied by a letter: "This is altogether superior to all save two or three poems in the entire range of American poetry," and signed EDGAR ALLAN POE. (Since he was never legally adopted Edgar had retained his own name as well as the impressive one so well-known in the South.)

The amused editor printed both poem and note, and added the comment, "If Edgar Allan Poe would but do himself justice he might make a beautiful and perhaps a magnificent poem. There is a good deal here to justify such a hope."

"Ah!" shouted the youth, "the very first words of encouragement I ever remember to have heard!" He shot off a copy of the *Gazette* to his guardian, and on the strength of the comment persuaded another publisher to bring out a collection of his poems. He received no cash, of course, but two hundred and fifty copies in payment. So, with *Al Aaraaf, Tamerlane, and Minor Poems,* Edgar Allan Poe became a published poet.

For years Edgar had been imploring his guardian: "My father, do not throw me aside as degraded. I will be an honor to your name. The world shall hear of the son whom you have thought unworthy of your notice." Occasionally a gift of a few dollars had resulted, but now, with something actually in print, the unworthy son was invited to come home.

Shabby but polished and brushed by his loving aunt, Mrs. Clemm, he returned to the luxurious house. Could he hope his impending West Point career had won his guardian's heart? Was he to be reinstated as the childless man's heir? He soon found out. After a few days there was another quarrel over his "idleness," and when the papers to West Point came he was packed off with a curt handshake and a pair of blankets.

West Point was unbearable from the first—its lack of privacy, of time to write, of intellectual companionship. And when Mr. Allan shortly took a young wife of the right age for producing heirs, Edgar saw no point in enduring it longer. Getting out was simple—he need just cut a few classes and drills—and in February, 1831, with a secondhand suit, cadet's overcoat, and one dollar in his pocket, he set out for New York.

At twenty-two Edgar Allan Poe had already developed his famous romantic look—black suit, flowing black hair, pallid skin and big melancholy eyes. Graced with a touching gentleness and a bewitching manner of speech, he had talked his classmates into subscribing seventy-five cents each for a new edition of his poems. Elam Bliss, who was to publish them, was the only person he knew in New York, but Edgar was too proud to show himself in his shabbiness, and from some hole he was living in he wrote a disjointed letter to his guardian: "I am confined to my bed . . . I have no money

. . . no friends . . . I have written my brother but he cannot help me. . . . Besides a most violent cold on my lungs my ear discharges blood and my headache is distracting. Please send me a little money quickly. God bless you. I shall send to the post office every day."

After a long fruitless wait he finally went to Mr. Bliss, who invited him to dinner and lent him a little money. For three months this man was Edgar's only contact with the human spirit, and the bitter winter left the poet permanently damaged, for his heart never recovered from the tension and starvation. At last he fled back to Mrs. Clemm.

Throughout his entire life—his tragic marriage later, his drinking and use of drugs, his pitiful and ridiculous love affairs—this woman was his granite support, nursing him in sickness, encouraging and protecting him in adversity. Puritan in dress, with square, unbeautiful face and weary eyes, she trudged with a basket on her arm from neighbor to neighbor, never quite begging but always managing to come home with something. Through her the wretched household survived.

At the Clemms', Edgar nursed his dying brother and wrote far into the night. He had been submitting stories—once with a pathetic note, "I am poor"—but without result. Then the Baltimore *Saturday Visitor* announced a contest, $50 for the best short story and $25 for a poem, and on October 12, 1833, the editors published their decision: *Edgar Allan Poe has submitted six tales, all distinguished by a wild, vigorous and poetical imagination, a rich style, a fertile invention and varied and curious learning. We have chosen "Ms. Found in a Bottle."*

The discerning judges had pinpointed his attributes precisely, missing only the power of analysis that later was to distinguish the detective stories.

This $50 prize was a turning point of sorts, for it brought him to the attention of newspaper editors. The *Southern*

Literary Messenger, Richmond, Virginia, bought some of his stories, and after two years engaged him at $10 a week to select contributions, write reviews, and supply original stories; in short, to be the editor. He went to Richmond gratefully, and his reviews, though frequently cruel, displayed taste and learning, and under his hand the circulation soared. So did his salary—to $15. It was the first taste of monetary success.

During this time John Allan died, and Edgar learned in dismay that he was not even mentioned in his former guardian's will. Furthermore, when he tried to enter his old home the young widow refused him the door. So now Mrs. Clemm and his twelve-year-old cousin Virginia, were truly his only refuge. Till recently Virginia had been the cherished little "Sissy," but with adolescence her waxen beauty and innocence began exerting a new attraction, neither wholly sensual nor wholly intellectual but as strong as the two combined.

Mrs. Clemm took note of the change. With her son Henry gone to sea, "Grandma" Poe and Edgar's brother dead, and the pension no more, she found herself left with no one but Virginia. And even Virginia might be torn from her, for some Poe relatives, suspicious of Edgar's intentions, had offered to take the girl in. She wrote to Edgar asking his advice.

His answer was a drunken wail: "I love Virginia devotedly. Now I shall never behold her again. My agony is more than I can bear. You have driven me to the grave. God have mercy on me, what have I to live for, among strangers with not one soul to love me. How can you be so cruel? I cannot advise you. Ask Virginia, let her write me herself bidding me goodbye. Then my heart will break but I will say no more."

Beside himself, he followed his hysterical letter to Baltimore and, on September 22, 1835, took out a marriage license. No wedding ceremony was ever recorded, and if there was one it was kept a deep secret. But Mrs. Clemm and Virginia joined him in Richmond, and a year and a half later, when she was fourteen, there was a formal wedding, with a two-week honeymoon.

This marriage can be explained only by the very special circumstances: Virginia was a sweet, pliable girl anxious to please those she loved, and not only Edgar but her mother desired the marriage. As for Poe, this obsession was only part of a larger mental disorder. Be it said, however, that his devotion to Virginia, as she sickened and died little by little, was genuine and touching, and she lives on in some of his most haunting work—"Ligeia," "Eulalie," "Eleanora," "Morella," "Berenice," "Annabel Lee."

Despite Poe's success with the *Messenger*, his drinking increased unaccountably after his marriage, and following one Christmastime explosion he was dismissed. Word of his editorial ability had spread, however, and he was invited to edit the *Gentleman's Magazine* in Philadelphia. There for a time he actually kept the two women in some comfort.

Earning a salary by day, he spent his nights working on his extraordinary stories. But masterpieces though they were, they alone never supported him. The prevailing copyright laws permitted American publishers to bring out English novels without paying their authors royalties, and the average novelist in the United States was unable to compete except on starvation terms. Unknowns therefore had to concentrate on short stories for the magazines, and Poe dreamed of starting one of his own, to be called the *Penn Magazine*. This tantalizing pot of gold beckoned to him from the rainbow's end for the rest of his life.

Though as an editor he frequently incurred libel suits by his careless charges of plagiarism, and drank and quarreled his way out of several positions, his brilliance was recognized increasingly and as one magazine dropped him another picked him up. Under his hand one publication's circulation reached forty thousand copies, the country's largest at the time, and his salary went to $800 a year, with extra payment for stories of his own. There was a pleasant cottage for the three of them, and for Virginia pretty clothes and a piano and harp. During this period, Mr. and Mrs. Edgar Allan Poe dined at some of the town's nicest homes (while, characteristically, Mrs. Clemm waited for them in the host's kitchen to collect the remains of the feast and to help guide Edgar safely home past the doors of saloons).

It was at this point that the world experienced something new in fiction—"Ligeia," "The Telltale Heart," "The Fall of the House of Usher," "Morella," "William Wilson." Through these hair-raising narratives Poe revealed his nightmare fascination with violence and death, his opium fantasies and, most significant, his dread of insanity. Readers were both revolted and enthralled by them, and though his personal profit was slight—"Ligeia" brought him $10—the magazines that published them prospered mightily.

At the same time, Poe was developing his peculiar power of solving mysteries by reasoning from effect backwards to cause. "The Murders in the Rue Morgue" deals with the violent death of a woman (again the woman-death theme) and the step-by-step uncovering of the killer. It was literature's first real murder-mystery or whodunit, and the character of Auguste Dupin the detective (Poe himself, of course), the first Sherlock Holmes. It created a sensation.

Later he based "The Mystery of Marie Roget" on New York City newspaper reports of the unsolved murder of a certain Cecilia Rogers, and in working out his plot actually identified the real murderer.

During this period his pursuing demons seemed to have forgotten him and all was serene. Virginia at eighteen was a dazzling beauty with high wide forehead, large violet eyes and a magnolia skin. Poe idolized her with a feverish rapture, and she responded with tenderness and trust. Then in January, 1842, the demons pounced again. One evening while Virginia was playing the harp and singing for a few friends a sudden hemorrhage of the lungs occurred. Tuberculosis, "the white plague," had taken Edgar's mother and brother, and now the sentence had fallen on his beloved wife.

He went temporarily out of his mind, imagining her already dead. "I felt all the agonies of her death," he said later, "and I became insane, with long intervals of horrible sanity. During the fits of unconsciousness I drank, God only knows how often and how much." This was only the first of many such dreaded crises.

In this drunken state he quarreled with associates and neglected his duties. The magazine's owner, George Graham, tried sympathizing with him, reasoning, and finally, threatening, but to no avail. After one long absence Poe returned to find another man at his desk. Without a word he wheeled around and walked out.

Anxiety again gripped the little cottage. Mrs. Clemm returned to her sewing and begging, and after selling their piano they moved to a smaller house. But now Poe was off in pursuit of his *Penn Magazine* again. Thomas Clark of the *Saturday Evening Post* had shown interest in backing it; a friend in Washington had said he would take Poe to the President's son; together they might get President Tyler's endorsement and thus drum up subscriptions. Poe, afire with excitement over the prospect, begged Clark for train fare and with it made for the capital.

Tension had always unsteadied him, and now, by tragic mischance, when he got to Washington the friend was ill and innocently turned him over to a certain convivial character known as Rowdy Dow. The inevitable happened, and next morning Poe could not even pay for a shave. He and Rowdy Dow did go through a number of government offices asking for subscriptions to the magazine, but Dow balked at showing him at the White House. That night Poe wrote Clark begging for ten dollars, as usual sacrificing accuracy to effect: "All is going right. I have got the subscriptions of *all* the departments, President, etc. I believe I am making a sensation which will benefit the magazine." Sensation, yes; benefit, question mark.

He had gone about the city shouting, waving his arms, insisting on wearing his cape turned inside out, and ended in a fracas when he made noisy fun of a Spanish gentleman with an oversized moustache. Dow wrote Clark: "I feel it my duty to write you concerning E.A.P. He has been, at intervals, quite unreliable. I think it advisable for you to come and see him safely back home. Mrs. Poe is in a bad state of health, and I charge you, as you have a soul to save, to say not one word to her. Should you not come we will see him on board the cars for Philadelphia. I do this under a solemn responsibility. Mr. Poe has the highest order of intellect, and I cannot suffer him to injure himself here. . . ." It was of course poor Mrs. Clemm who took charge of him in Philadelphia, and though he made light of the affair to his friends, this was the end of Mr. Clark's backing.

As he destroyed himself he turned on others, venting his frustration in biting book reviews that only multiplied his enemies. "The Gold Bug," memento of those days at Fort Moultrie, and "The Black Cat," reeking with senseless cruelty, were almost all he sold for a whole year.

All this time he had been working on "The Raven," which, though it was to become his masterpiece, was first to bring him his most galling experience. Poe often left to the piteous Mrs. Clemm the peddling of his wares, but one day when there was not a crumb in the house he himself went to his old editor, Graham, who still bought an occasional poem. Trembling, he held out a roll of blue paper. (He prided himself on his picturesque handwriting, and with dying Virginia's help had pasted the pages together into one long sheet.) Graham read to the end. Then slowly and sadly he shook his head and handed it back.

Poe nearly broke down. "The poem is good," he pleaded.

"I know it is good. But even if it isn't, for God's sake have mercy. My beloved wife is starving, and you know how ill she is. My mother-in-law is a saint, who performs miracles in feeding us, but we have nothing now, nothing. If I come home empty-handed we will die."

The kindly Graham sent for his staff. "Read it aloud to them," he said, and in the poet's magnificent voice the sonorous phrases rolled forth: "Nevermore . . . nevermore." At the end there was an embarrassed silence and at last the editor, aching with pity, gently took down a hat, dropped in a bill and passed it to the next man. Each mutely added a bill.

Poe, too desperate to refuse the fifteen dollars, and too hurt to acknowledge it, stuffed the poem into his pocket and crept from the room with eyes averted. It was his life's worst moment—thus far.

Philadelphia, where these things happened to him, had become unbearable, and finally, with his last eleven dollars, he dragged the trusting Virginia to New York, leaving Mrs. Clemm to sell the furniture and follow with Catarina, the cat. Come to roost in a farmhouse near what is now Broadway and 84th Street, Poe exorcised his death fears in "The Premature Burial" and "The Oblong Box" and continued polishing "The Raven," while Mrs. Clemm made numberless calls on the New York *Mirror*. With her pitiful accounts of her dying daughter and ill son-in-law, she persuaded the editor to give Poe a minor job.

As a further favor the editor paid him ten dollars and printed his poem. The result was one of those literary explosions rarely achieved by a piece of poetry, for scores of other papers copied it; it was published abroad and discussed and argued over. Suddenly everyone was "raven-mad," and Poe found himself asked to give readings and lectures; a collection of his tales was published with royalties actually paid to him—at eight cents a copy. Finally, he was made editor of the *Broadway Journal* at a substantial salary.

Edgar Allan Poe

After the years of rebuffs, his starved ego went reeling drunkenly, and on being taken up by a group of starry-eyed poetesses with floating veils and smelling salts, he plunged from one infatuation to another, all of them very public and undignified. His lady-loves, morbidly fascinated by his haunted eyes and haggard features, saw in him the poet-lover they had never known; conversely, he saw in them his boyhood goddess, Mrs. Stanard, re-embodied. With them he exchanged sentimental poems which he printed, complete with identifying initials, in the *Journal*, for the double purpose of supplying material for the paper and inflaming the public's curiosity about EAP. These affairs were seldom as compromising as they sounded, but no one could know that, and he was soon the talk of New York.

Virginia and Mrs. Clemm watched in motherly amusement, realizing that these absurd exhibitions had no real meaning. Incapable of jealousy, Virginia invited his poetesses to the house, laughing quietly with Mrs. Clemm over some of their more ardent effusions, and Mrs. Clemm continued to scrub and beg and act as nurse as loyally as ever.

Still, all this notoriety and hard work failed to be converted into money, for though numerous magazines prospered on his writings there was then no law to compel them to pay for what they printed, and again out of work and starving, Poe took his two women to a tiny cottage in Fordham that was to be their last home together. In this bare shack they reached the deepest pit of poverty. Gleamingly clean it always was, but during the terrible winter of 1847 Virginia lay on a bed with only straw for mattress and only Edgar's West Point overcoat for cover, hugging Catarina the cat to her breast for warmth while the others held her icy hands and feet. One of the poetesses, discovering them thus, rushed back to New York to spread the pitiful story.

At once the *Morning Express* took up the alarm: "We regret to learn that Edgar Allan Poe and his wife are both dangerously ill and that the hand of misfortune lies heavy

upon their temporal affairs. We hope the friends and ad-
mirers of Mr. Poe will come promptly to his assistance in his
bitterest hour of need." His magazine friends looked the
other way, but the poetesses managed to scrape together
sixty dollars.

Poe stood watch by Virginia's bed in anguish. Each spasm
of coughing seemed as though it must be her last, and each
time he went temporarily out of his mind. Virginia was
haunted by anxiety for him: "Eddie dear," she pleaded,
"when I am gone, put your hands over your head, so, and
I will be there to shield you." To Mrs. Clemm she cried:
"Darling, darling Muddy, you will take care of my poor
Eddie? You will never leave him? Promise me; then I can
die in peace."

At last her day of leaving came. On January 30, 1847, Mrs.
Marie Shew, the kindest of the poetesses, sat beside her.
Drawing from under her pillow a picture of Edgar, and his
mother's jewel box, Virginia asked the friend to read aloud
two letters written long ago by Mrs. Allan, his foster mother,
which cleared him of blame in the Allan family quarrels.
That night she died and was laid in the vault of a friend, her
husband having no money for a grave.

Virginia gone, Poe collapsed, mind and body; and while
he recovered physically, his actions thereafter betrayed the
mental deterioration. Pursued by irrational terrors, he
clutched at any refuge. The eternal cry "Give me love" was
answered by one woman after another who did not know he
was seeking only escape from reality, and so confused did
he become that at one time he was vowing eternal devotion
to one woman while drawing up a marriage contract with
another. All these affairs were the actions of a deranged mind
and had no more significance than the ugly dreams of
delirium.

At times his heart weakened and he seemed near death,
and even Mrs. Clemm, the woman of granite, began to

despair. "I wish we were both in our graves," she moaned. "God knows it would be best." Then, when everything was at its blackest, a shaft of sunshine cleft the gloom. An unknown admirer in the Midwest wrote offering to finance Poe in a magazine. Hail to the old dream come to life once more!

Hail, moreover, to escape from New York's horrors. Hail to Richmond, his spiritual home. Instructing the eager Midwesterner to mail a fifty-dollar advance to Richmond, he packed his carpetbag. But Mrs. Clemm was strangely foreboding despite his cheery reassurance, "Don't fear for your Eddie, I'll be good while I'm away. I'll come back to love and comfort you." She never saw him again.

It was two weeks before he arrived in Richmond. He had been found wandering the streets of Philadelphia in wild flight from imaginary enemies. His dementia was mistaken for a drunken frenzy and he had been taken to jail, where someone recognized him as the famous poet. He was released with ten dollars and sent on to Richmond. From there he wrote Mrs. Clemm: "I got here with two dollars, of which I enclose you one. Oh God, Mother, if you could come to me! Shall we ever meet again? If possible, oh, *come!* My clothes are so *horrible* and I am so *ill.* Oh, if you *could* come to me, *my mother!*" One dollar would not bring her and, living on the charity of one of his poetesses, she had to remain behind.

Then, again, better times were upon him. He had appealed to the Mackenzies, who were still sheltering his sister Rosalie, and they had supplied his barest needs. But he was famous now, and Richmond was glad to welcome her celebrated son. Ancient scandals had lost their bite and some of the city's finest houses were opened to him. The younger generation was fascinated by this handsome black-clad poet, erect and slender, with soft voice and gentle manner. He was invited to lecture and read his remarkable "Raven"—even, occasionally, for pay.

He also renewed acquaintance with his boyhood sweetheart Elmira, now the rich and handsome widow, Mrs. Barrett Shelton. Their betrayed love affair had made a deep scar on both, and when they met, the air was electric with expectation. Soon Elmira and he were engaged and the marriage date set. He assured Mrs. Clemm: "I think she loves me more devotedly than I ever knew, and I cannot help loving her in return."

The next three months were a bright sunset after a stormy day. Elmira's social position would blot out the early years of his ignominy, while her fortune would finance the magazine (the Midwesterner having proved balky over details). Indeed, so rosy had everything become, so altered was he, that at her urging he pledged himself to stop drinking and to join the Sons of Temperance.

August and September of 1849 passed happily. It is true that he was still penniless (poor Mrs. Clemm had had nothing since the dollar in June) but that too was suddenly mended, for a Mr. St. Leon Loud offered Poe the greatest single sum he had ever earned, a hundred dollars, to edit his wife's poems. So now he could close the cottage in New York and bring "Muddy" back to live with Elmira and himself.

The day before he left for New York a friend remarked on his gaiety of spirit. For once his poverty seemed to lie lightly, and he accepted a five-dollar loan with a gentle smile, saying, "You have been very kind to me. Here is a little trifle that may be worth something to you." Diffidently he proffered a small roll of paper in his beautiful handwriting, the poem "Annabel Lee."

A few hours later his mind broke. At four in the morning, without bidding Elmira goodbye, he boarded a ship, and on arriving in Baltimore disappeared for five days. On October 3 a doctor acquaintance received a penciled note:

DEAR SIR:
There is a gentleman rather the worse for wear, at Ryan's 4th ward polls, who goes under the cognomen of Edgar A.

Poe, and who appears in great distress, and he says he is acquainted with you, and I assure you, he is in need of immediate assistance.

Yours, in haste,

Jos. W. WALKER

He had been found lying on the sidewalk, his clothes filthy and torn to rags. At the hospital, he could not recall his address or relatives' names, and he kept up a delirious chatter with imaginary objects creeping up the walls. When he became sane again, the doctor cheerily promised to have him up and about in a few days, but Poe cried in a loud voice: "No, no. The best thing you could do would be to blow out my brains." Four days he kept moaning and shouting, sometimes struggling violently to get up and then quietly subsiding. At last he muttered, "Lord help my poor soul," and his tortured heart gave out.

Mrs. Clemm learned of her Eddie's death from the newspapers. For a while she hoped to receive royalties from his books, but like him, she was doomed to poverty and ended her days on the charity of his poetesses.

In the following years all these women, and many men calling themselves his friends, had their say about Poe in print. Some made him out a devil; others vehemently tried to whitewash the facts altogether. But the truth was simply that he was a genius tormented by alcoholism, an illness too little understood in his time.

Genius he certainly was, with a unique influence on many who came after. Quoted and argued over, his eerie poems and stories inspired a whole new school of writers and painters, and the art of Edgar Allan Poe brought new stature to American letters on both sides of the Atlantic.

Charles Dickens

(1812=1870)

Charles Dickens

(1812-1870)

THE Queen had been waiting for him, and when he entered she extended her pudgy hand with a smile: "We are pleased to welcome you, Mr. Dickens. Your books and readings have given us great pleasure."

They were a trifle shy at first, this little woman, empress of millions of souls, and the handsome man with millions of followers of his own. But considering the difference in their beginnings, they got on together amazingly well. Because, as a matter of protocol, visitors never sat in the royal presence, she paid him the unusual compliment of standing while they talked, and she invited him and his daughter to her next reception. When he left she gave him a copy of her personal memoirs inscribed, *From one of the humblest of authors to one of the greatest—Victoria Regina.*

In the Queen such humility was breathtaking, but it scarcely made Charles Dickens blink, for he had been accustomed to this kind of thing for twenty-five years. Indeed, his story is without parallel, in that, though most writers have a failure now and then just to keep them steady, failure was one experience he missed altogether. From his earliest effort, *Sketches by Boz,* through *A Tale of Two Cities* and "A Christmas Carol" to *David Copperfield, Great Expectations,* and finally, *Edwin Drood,* there were nearly twenty books with not a miscarriage among them.

His private life also was unusual. Though the Victorian era was notable for a certain solemnity, this genius of laughter was its most beloved son, and his popularity survived even some quite un-Victorian behavior. He was too charming, too amusing, to be bound by ordinary rules.

Thus transcending the limitations of his time, he was still peculiarly *of* those times. He experienced the full range of English life, from slum to castle, and the best and the worst of each. Most of his experiences went into his books, so that the reader, while laughing at his fiction, is reading his biography as well. Glimpses of it appear in *Oliver Twist* and *Great Expectations*—the loneliness and poverty in one, the ambition and youthful snobbery in the other. In *David Copperfield* one finds the whole personality. His parents are there too, posturing absurdly as Mr. and Mrs. Micawber; but some of these scenes he never acknowledged as his own, for the strain of pride was very strong in him.

Dickens was born in 1812 in the south England town of Portsea. His parents were happily married, and for a few years their six children were happy too. There was a comfortable home with games in the parlor of an evening, and plenty of everything to make life agreeable. To Charles it was clear that his father, with his grand speech, his burnished top hat and his manner of gracing the air with his presence, was unequaled among men for wit and splendor. Moreover, there was some delicious relationship between the Dickens family and a duke; the details were fuzzy, but, no question, the head of the house was as magnificent as any duke, as kind, as cheery—and, of course, as rich. When Charles grew up he too would be rich, famous, important. A mansion nearby named Gad's Hill, being to him the world's handsomest house, would be his to live in. Like everything else desirable, it would be his just for the asking.

Slowly, at eight, his eyes began to open. He became conscious of his mother fluttering and moaning over something

CHARLES DICKENS

called *bills* that had to be met and weren't, and his father promising to make them all wealthy just as soon as something worth considering turned up. Finally, Mr. Dickens decided this happy event was more likely to take place in London, and the family's belongings were piled into boxes and made ready for moving.

At this moment Charles's world collapsed. During the next seven or eight years he suffered such misery that the entire rest of his life was one prodigious effort to make up to himself for it. His teacher had begged Mr. Dickens to let the bright little boy finish out the school term, and when the stagecoach clattered away with the family inside he was left standing on the curb, alone and terrified. For the rest of the term he was numb with loneliness. Then, when he rejoined them there were further shocks. Mr. Dickens still strutted about as grandly as ever, but behind its closed shutters their shabby house was barren of furniture, and the bill collectors kept shouting insults through the keyhole. Now the full truth became apparent: the Dickenses' awesome relationship with the duke was simply Gran'pa Dickens' tenure as His Grace's butler; Mr. Dickens himself, furthermore, was a foolish, good-hearted bag of hot wind and Mrs. Dickens a featherbrain too distracted by her brood to give them the care they craved. Worst of all, it seemed that he, Charles, was not even worthy of an education. Skin crawling with shame, he wandered the streets day after day like a homeless dog, enviously watching the other children on their way to school.

Three years of this empty misery endured; then Mr. Dickens met the owner of a shoeblacking factory and the misery worsened. Blacking came in pots which had to be wrapped and labeled—just the job, Mr. Dickens thought, to keep an idle twelve-year-old out of mischief, while his salary of six shillings a week would lift the family's spirits remarkably. So Charles found himself slinking down a waterfront alley to a warehouse alive with rats and young hoodlums who jeered at his clean clothes and delicate speech. Loathing every moment of it, he was shown how to wrap a blue label around a pot and clip it on securely. Worse, being too proud to let it defeat him, he learned the job so well that to his horror he was put to do it in a street window like a performing circus animal.

His working days were eleven-hour nightmares, and since his own parents were responsible, there was no one to turn to for help. Indeed, as he was bent over his pots one day he saw his father outside watching, apparently unperturbed by his son's humiliating situation. How, Charles wondered, could he endure to see him thus shamed?

In truth Mr. Dickens had other worries to occupy him, for his creditors were running out of patience, and finally they cast him into debtor's prison. Marshalsea was no ordinary jail, however; the inmates could wander about, play games, even set up housekeeping, and before long Mrs. Dickens, sobbing dramatically, moved in with the younger children, bag and baggage.

This was the bleakest time of all. His mother had fluttered off without bothering about a room for him, but he found one for himself in a dismal lodging house. After performing like a talented monkey all day at the factory, he went to Marshalsea for supper and then home through the black streets. The misery of these days was never forgotten, and he described them unforgettably in *David Copperfield.* But so ashamed of them was he that neither his wife nor his children, none but the one friend who later became his biographer, was ever told that it had all actually happened to him.

For once Mr. Dickens' optimistic predictions came true, and something did turn up in the shape of a small inheritance from a relative, which bought him his freedom. Then Charles's luck turned too, for his father quarreled with the blacking manufacturer and he was fired forthwith. There was a terrible moment when his worried mother argued for patching up the quarrel (he said later, "I shall never forget, I never can forget, that she was warm for my being sent back"). This time, however, his father plumped for school, thereby earning his affection and support forever.

Mr. Jones' Classical and Commercial Academy was not much of a school, but after jail and the blacking pots it was heaven, and Charles stayed there two years, an ordinary boy at ordinary tasks, only rather more high-spirited, handsome, friendly, hard-working and intelligent than most. But dreadful poverty was always snapping at his heels, and once he had grabbed an education he knew he must be on his way. At sixteen, he went to work in a lawyer's office. Such employment was too confining for this restless spirit, and after studying shorthand at night he became a newspaper reporter.

By the age of eighteen a lifelong characteristic was already evident—his gift for friendship. He was a born companion, interested in everyone, listening, enjoying prodigiously, envying not at all. Because he liked his father he trusted men, and of his countless men friends he never permanently lost one. Women, on the other hand, were always a problem to him, beginning with his mother's betrayal. And now, after two lonely years in "rooms," the penniless youth went with a friend straight to disaster.

It would have been well for Charles if they had gone anywhere but to the house of Mr. George Beadnell, for the Beadnells had three young daughters. The family was polite enough, though unimpressed by the new caller, but he was impressed enough for all. Not only were the Beadnells well-off and the girls pretty, the prettiest of all, twenty-one-year-old Maria, was a flirt. She struck him dumb with love.

Maria was the first of numerous destructive women in Charles's life and he later painted her twice in deathless (and deadly) literary portraits. Of all such unfortunate relationships, this was the most damaging, for though he begged and stormed her heart, she kept him dangling for four years. This obscure young man was no husband for a Beadnell, and finally she flounced off to Paris, leaving him broken-hearted.

Losing her was anguish enough—the blow to his pride struck even deeper. Cover up the wound as he might, it refused to heal, and twenty-five years later he was still blanching at the mention of her name. However, the heartbreak served him well, for like poverty it drove him to seek solace in success. Reporting by day, he threw himself into amateur theatricals by night and, foreshadowing later stage triumphs, acted, wrote and directed with frantic verve. Acting even attracted him as a profession, but luckily for the world a sore throat interfered with a crucial audition and he remained with the newspaper. Soon he was one of London's best reporters, no story too hard to get, no fact too small to record. Galloping about the countryside, writing notes on his palm when his paper ran out, he exhausted himself and his horse bringing back the story, and his exuberant shout, "First! I'm first again!" was a regular sound in the office.

During these days of scouring the country he witnessed the manifold evils he later exposed so relentlessly. The crime-breeding poverty in *Oliver Twist,* the delays of the law in *Bleak House,* the heartless official red tape in *Little Dorrit,* the shame of public charity in *Our Mutual Friend,* the brutalities in boys' schools in *Nicholas Nickelby,* these evils and others were brought to public attention so vividly that he became one of the most effective reformers of the day.

For several years reporting seemed like glorious fun. Yet there was one drawback—one had to be too accurate, there could be no embroidering the facts to make them more entertaining. Now his real talent emerged, the ability to depict everything larger and funnier than life. Down he sat one fall evening in 1833 and scribbled a sketch about some comical people he had met. Laughing, he let his imagination run wild, then folded the paper and walked to the *Monthly*

Magazine in Fleet Street. The office door being locked, he dropped it through the letter slot, characteristically never doubting that it would be accepted. Characteristically, it was, instantly.

This was the first of *Sketches by Boz*. It was followed by another and another, each attracting more attention to "Boz." Later the manager of a rival periodical asked Charles to write for that paper; he also asked him to dinner. And taking one thing with another, this probably makes Mr. George Hogarth the most generous person in Charles Dickens' life, for he introduced him not only to a job but to three of the most important people in his life.

Mr. Hogarth had fourteen children, including the three daughters, Kate, Mary and Georgina. Kate was nineteen, small and fairly pretty, with curls bouncing about her cheeks. Her temper was even, her nature slow and docile. Unfortunately, she was not very bright, being notable chiefly for rather silly puns.

Mary was fifteen, a gentle child serene in the conviction that the whole world was as good and gentle as herself. Mary loved everyone and everyone loved her—and to cap the miracle, she was almost if not quite a beauty.

Georgina was a mere seven. All anyone noticed about her at present was that she was not as pretty as the others but was very efficient about the house.

The Hogarths' welcome was warmer than the Beadnells', for Charles had more polish now and a surer reputation; moreover, his good looks, his amusing stories, his gaiety, made him an attractive addition to the circle. He had buried the memory of Maria Beadnell as deeply as he could, and now, turning from the painful past, on a wild rebound he proposed to the Hogarth sister of the most suitable age.

The marriage between Kate and Charles was a hopeless mismatch, its only bonds being a mutual readiness for the state of matrimony and a certain physical attraction. For

Kate, it was like colliding with a hurricane. A simple breeze can be stood up to, but faced with an elemental force of nature, one must either lie flat and let it pass over, or ride the heavens with it. Kate was incapable of flight. But Charles did not know it at the time, and in April, 1838, she became his wife.

Shortly before the marriage—indeed, making it financially possible—a firm of publishers had offered him fourteen pounds a month to write a serial about the adventures of a group of travelers. The characters had to be likable and amusing enough to hold the reader's attention month after month, and Charles, accepting confidently, began *The Posthumous Papers of the Pickwick Club.*

The success of *Pickwick* was unlike anything hitherto known in literature. The Fat Boy went into the language; there were Pickwick hats, coats, canes and cigars, while half the pets in England answered to Dowler, Sam, Jingle, Trotter, or Winkle. Its effect was to bring him a flood of other offers, and with his abundance of energy he began two other serials, turning out monthly installments of all three. Simultaneously he wrote the libretto of an opera and edited a magazine.

No one ever enjoyed his success more than did Dickens—unless it was his friends. He was intoxicated by it, and everyone exposed to his buoyant vivacity and openhanded hospitality caught the excitement. Jaunty in velvet jacket, colorful waistcoat and wide white hat perched on his rich flowing hair, he was the dandy incarnate—a shade overdone, perhaps, but so disarmingly happy no one could carp. "What a face is his to meet in a drawing room," exclaimed a new artist friend. "It has the life and soul of fifty human beings."

Dickens had, too, the eyes and ears of fifty, absorbing everything at once, comic, pathetic, dramatic, factual. Though attacked often by illness he never once let it interfere with either pleasure or work, in a superabundance of energy often leaving a coach to walk beside the horses or, from sheer spirits, letting out a joyous whoop in a quiet London street. Till the time of his death he dragged his friends on interminable walks in all weathers. "I was out of spirits and energy today," he once complained. "I could scarcely walk ten miles."

As soon as the money began pouring in, Charles rented a comfortable house at 18 Doughty Place. Already devoted to Kate's young sister, the gentle Mary, he proposed that she come to live with them, and she was ensconced in a small room at the head of the stairs. Now seventeen, this bright, intelligent girl was a complete contrast to Charles's robust earthiness, for though quick to respond to his every idea and mood she was somehow remote and otherworldly. A strange radiance filled any place she entered, and he was not the only one to call her a saint.

In time Kate gave birth to a son—Charles Jr.—and everything at Doughty Place was ideal. With a fine home, success, a beautiful heir and the two women he loved most (the unforgotten Maria Beadnell was a dim unacknowledged ache), how could Charles be less than happy? Then one day without a trace of warning Mary died, quietly and uncomplainingly, of a heart disease no one had ever known she had.

Charles himself came near dying, and for two months his mind seemed paralyzed. He had not loved this girl as a sweetheart, but as something altogether holy and unblemished. Like a talisman he wore her little ring for life, and many years afterwards he cried, "She is in my thoughts at all times. The recollection is an essential part of my being, as inseparable as the beating of my heart." His later years were a feverish search for the harmony she had represented, and if he had found it he might have avoided the tragic mistakes that tarnished his bright career.

For two months he could write nothing, but as athletes must exercise, so writers must write, and he got back to his desk, finding relief from his pain through *The Old Curiosity Shop* and its Little Nell. So poignantly did he express his emotions that when the book began appearing in serial form its readers were equally affected: As Little Nell's death drew near and the next installment was due in Boston, four thousand persons gathered on the dock to meet the boat.

"Is Little Nell dead?" they called as it approached.

"Yes," the captain called back, and a great groan filled the waterfront.

Having wrung all hearts as Little Nell, Mary kept reappearing in his books: as Amy in *Little Dorrit,* Florence in *Dombey and Son,* Agnes in *David Copperfield,* Rose in *Oliver Twist.* Truth to tell, though no one else pervaded his novels as she did, most of his friends and acquaintances served him in them at least once. His mind was a squirrel's nest of eccentric mannerisms and quaint personalities which he later brought out with such names as Peggotty or Sairy Gamp or Uriah Heep. His plots might be overdrawn at times, his villains too black or his Mary-heroines too candy-pink, but the vitality of the man never flagged, the invention never failed. Even his one departure into historical fiction, *A Tale of Two Cities,* was such vivid drama that his customary comedy is barely missed.

As with many authors under examination, the striving years of youth seem the most interesting, for a continuous list of triumphs lacks the thrill of suspense. Dickens' career provided little in the way of failure to relieve the monotony of success, save when he toured the United States and wrote *American Notes*; his blasts at slavery did not charm American readers, but even this disfavor was short-lived, for in time they themselves shared his views and all was cordiality again.

In his own prosperity he took on numberless activities in behalf of others. He gave a fortune to charities and raised other fortunes for needy actors and authors by performing brilliantly in amateur theatricals. With equal force he lectured on political, ethical, artistic, social, and literary questions, and if his opinions were not always sound, his enthusiasm was always infectious.

Still, his enormous earnings were not always adequate. Kate and he had nine children, and expenses often outran income. Then, he simply worked harder. Always the actor (he said once, "There is nothing in the world equal to seeing the audience rise to you, one sea of delighted faces, one hurrah of applause"), he put his hobby into harness and made a second fortune reading from his own books. Now more than ever he was feted by celebrities and fawned on by celebrity-hunters; he joined the clubs of intellectuals and ate the dinners of duchesses. Eventually he fulfilled his oldest dream when he heard that Gad's Hill, the castle of his eight-year-old heart, was for sale. Buying it, he became at last a country gentleman.

Like every great man he had his biographers, and it was John Forster who first revealed that David Copperfield was Charles Dickens himself and that David's Dora was Charles's Maria Beadnell. He revealed also Charles's strange revenge: Charles had never forgotten Maria's humiliating rejection of him, but in recreating the love affair in *David Copperfield* he took a slight liberty with fact. In the book Dora (Maria), instead of coldly rejecting David (Charles), accepts him eagerly—then later humbly admits her own unworthiness. Psychologists would call this a wish-fulfillment, and indeed he may have thus salved the wound a little. Still, it was not altogether healed. That happened a quarter of a century afterwards, and then she herself did it for him.

For Mr. Charles Dickens a note arrived one day signed by Mrs. Maria Beadnell Winter. At sight of the name he nearly fainted, and, once more eighteen years old, he was ready to begin loving her all over again. He arranged a private meeting and waited, shaking, for her to enter. She bounced in.

Overdressed and underwitted, she gushed and giggled and simpered, and in half an hour a lifetime of heartache was cured. But being a writer, Charles could not let it rest there. Into *Little Dorrit* he slipped Mrs. Flora Finching, a widow who clucks and chatters like a middle-aged bantam hen. Not mean, not unpleasant, she comes off merely as absurd and not at all romantic. Thus he achieved his little private revenge.

This was in his forties. He was "the most astonishingly successful writing man in the English-speaking world," with a gift, it seemed, for turning everything he touched into gold. He took rowdy delight in his children and was adored by them in return; offstage and on, a sea of delighted faces always surrounded him, from the Queen's on down. But by this time dissatisfaction was setting in. The intense energy that had powered him was beginning to roar meaninglessly, like an engine out of control. "This unspeakable restless something," he cried, "this vague craving for something undefined, that nothing can satisfy!" He could not stay still, walked ten, twenty, thirty miles a day; he took a studio to work in, couldn't work, left it and went home. He made engagements and broke them, played games till he dropped, gave dramatic readings that left him gasping with exhaustion. Feverishly he explored slums, criminal courts, asylums, seeking through sensation to fill his emptiness. Maria's ghost was laid, but the disorder remained; he yearned with a ferocious hunger for something he could not name.

One thing he did know, Kate was not the answer to his craving. As the years went on, his dissatisfaction with her had increased. She had made dogged efforts to join him on his emotional flights, but what woman could keep up with Charles Dickens, especially when she had another child every second year? Untidy and helpless, she was never able to converse brilliantly or run a decent home, and at social functions she pulled herself into a corner like a bundle of old clothes. From embarrassment he had gone to irritation, then to total disregard for her, finally turning the management of the house over to her sister Georgina, who became his house-keeper and companion.

As he, then the house, and finally the children slipped from her grasp, Kate endured the humiliation patiently. For some time she had been meekly suggesting they might be better apart, but he was mindful of the Victorian convention that frowned on breaking up homes. Then, when he was forty-five, he met eighteen-year-old Ellen Ternan, an actress. "From that date," he confessed to his friend Wilkie Collins, "I have never known a moment's peace or content. There never was a man so seized and rended by one spirit."

In this new turmoil he found Kate unendurable, and they agreed to separate, one daughter going with her while Georgina and the other children remained with him. Against the advice of his friends, he made a statement to the papers defending his separation, and nothing could have carried him through the ensuing scandal but his country's long affection for him. Queen Victoria's invitation to a reception, recounted here earlier, came after the separation, and there was no slackening of his theatre audiences.

But the vague craving, the restlessness, were not to be satisfied. Ellen Ternan was a cold, mercenary girl (there are two characters, Estella in *Great Expectations* and Bella in *Our Mutual Friend,* whose natures, like their names, reflect hers) and he was tortured by jealousy and frustration. In desperation he took on more and more reading engagements. His doctors warned him of the strain on his heart but for too long he ignored them. Then he listened to medical advice and went back to Gad's Hill and to writing a new book.

On a June afternoon he sat working on *Edwin Drood.* He had written the words "scents from gardens, woods and fields penetrate into the Cathedral, subdue its earthly odor, and preach the Resurrection and the Life . . ." and at the end of the paragraph, inexplicably, he laid down his pen. A few hours later, like his beloved little Mary, he quickly and quietly died.

He had requested burial in the local church with no special fuss about it, but here the Queen intervened. On June 14, 1870, he was buried in Westminster Abbey, the proudest burial place in England, among poets and warriors and kings. As an old man accustomed to adulation he might not have regarded this honor as noticeably important, but certainly the boy Charles, wrapping paste pots in the factory window, would have taken great comfort from the manner of his last appearance.

The Brontës

Charlotte (1816=1855)
Emily (1818=1848)
Anne (1820=1849)

The Brontës

Charlotte (1816=1855)
Emily (1818=1848)
Anne (1820=1849)

Any day in the year 1821, one might have seen the door of
a gray stone house in Haworth, Yorkshire, open quietly
and a troop of children emerge, one four-year-old boy and
five girls, the oldest carrying the youngest pickaback. Sub-
dued by the haunting cries from the bedroom upstairs, they
would creep past the window where their father sat writing
and, picking a path among the gravestones, turn onto the
moor. There would be silence until they had left the parsonage behind, and then in a burst of spirits they would dash
off laughing. The treeless moors rolled away to the gray hori-
zon and the northern winds cut across the heather like a
scythe, but this was home to the Brontë children, and here
their hearts would turn until they died.

They would play at Catch for a while, shouting with
pleasure as the wind whipped their long skirts. Then, with
clothing sedately rearranged, they would troop back to the
dark house, to the uncarpeted floors and curtainless windows
and the moaning woman upstairs.

After many cruel months their mother died and the
stricken father was left to bring up his brood, a task for which
he had little talent or taste. The Reverend Patrick Brontë
had risen by hard work from an Irish farm to Cambridge
University, planning for himself a High Church career with a
sideline of writing. But somehow, the brilliant future had

ended in a dreary parsonage on the Yorkshire moor at two hundred pounds a year. His gentle, laughing wife Maria brought gaiety with her at first, and the six babies filled the house with cheerful noise, but gloom fell with her illness and death, and though her sister Branwell came north to run the house, he lost heart and ambition. Soon he was a recluse whose only pleasure was writing poetry.

Some years before, a dispute among the Haworth mill-workers had forced this stubbornly principled man to take an unpopular stand; thenceforth he always carried a pistol in self-protection and fired a few random shots out the window each morning to keep it in condition. This, and the habitual solitary walks, gave him a name for considerable eccentricity.

Eccentric Mr. Brontë was, but no ogre. Nor was Aunt Branwell a witch, despite her stark black dress, huge mobcap, and wooden overshoes clattering on the cold stone floors. They were simply two self-absorbed people totally unaware of the worth of the strange treasures entrusted to their care.

Of the six children, Elizabeth died too young to distinguish herself, but Charlotte and Emily were without question geniuses. Maria probably was one as well, while Branwell and Anne had indisputable talent. Their father gave the boy his lessons, but the others saw Mr. Brontë only at breakfast and tea, when he discoursed solemnly on literature or discussed with ten-year-old Maria the political topics of the day. From Aunt Branwell the girls received a smattering of the three R's, but for recreation the six crowded into one small room upstairs and there devoured Byron's romances, morbid religious tracts, London newspapers, and Gothic tales of blood and thunder. In the damp chill of this unheated room they developed the chronic chest trouble that was the lifetime plague of them all.

Without playmates other than the little animals of the moors, they knew no different life and were perfectly satis-

ANNE   EMILY   CHARLOTTE BRONTË

(from the painting by P. B. Brontë)

fied with things as they were. But in 1824, everything changed. Mr. Brontë, hard pressed to provide for his brood, heard of the inexpensive Cowan Bridge School for the Daughters of Impoverished Clergymen and to it thankfully packed off Maria, Elizabeth, Charlotte and Emily, respectively aged ten, nine, eight, and six.

Cowan Bridge left a lifelong scar on Charlotte, and years later she drew a shocking picture of it in *Jane Eyre*. In the novel, Lowood Orphan Asylum and its pious headmaster, its vengeful scourge-mistress and browbeaten pupils were all bitter reproductions of a dreadful reality. The food was uneatable, the house was damp and cold; during the first year nearly half the girls were found to have tuberculosis, and Elizabeth and the brilliant Maria (*Jane Eyre*'s Helen Burns) died.

After this disaster the next five years were spent entirely at home, during which time the foundations of the children's characters were laid. Tiny Charlotte, gray and fierce as a shrew, with nothing but magnificent eyes to redeem her plainness, was the family dynamo. Emily was already the individualist, handsome but detached and self-sufficient, while Branwell was the charmer and Anne the docile little follower-on. The one thing they all shared was imagination, and out of this sprang their extraordinary careers.

The novel-writing began in 1826, when Charlotte was ten. Mr. Brontë brought home a set of wooden soldiers to the nine-year-old Branwell, and Charlotte snatched up the biggest, crying, "This is the Duke of Wellington!" Emily commandeered one she called Gravey for his grave expression, and Anne's was a small thing like herself, Waiting-Boy. Branwell's, not surprisingly, was Buonaparte. They spent the day acting out a drama around the characters, and next day carried it further, sustaining this "Young Men's Play," as they called it, for many months.

"The Islanders" play was begun a year later. The four were

sitting chatting lazily with Tabby the cook, when Branwell yawned in boredom. "I wish there was something to do."

"You could all go to your beds," Tabby remarked dryly, but Charlotte ignored her and suggested dreamily, "Suppose we all had an island of our own?"

Branwell jumped at the notion. "If we had I'd choose the Isle of Man," he returned, and Charlotte went on, "Mine would be the Isle of Wight." Emily and Anne tossed in Arran and Guernsey, and the game was on at a gallop.

"We couldn't live there alone," Branwell mused, "we'd have to have other people. I'd pick the greatest, John Bull and Astley Cooper and Leigh Hunt." The others assembled their characters from the current news, and over the months "The Islanders" featured a spectacular series of wars, political intrigues, love affairs and slayings. In time, the original islands expanded into kingdoms and then continents; Charlotte and Branwell, closest in age and tastes, developed "Angria" while the other two collaborated on "Gondal." Imperceptibly this mental world became more absorbing, more truly real, than the uneventful routine of the parsonage. With no friends or outside amusements as counterbalance it was the supreme interest of their lives for ten or fifteen years, and when school separated them they carried it on by letter.

These were not inventions for a day, to be forgotten tomorrow. All four of the children being natural writers, they recorded them in hand-made books two or three inches square, over a hundred of which still survive, elaborately designed and containing up to twenty thousand words. So minute is the writing that a microscope is required to decipher it.

Many Brontë readers have wondered where these secluded girls found their highly charged plots, but the fact is that melodrama had always been their daily meat. Added to their early reading were their father's bloody tales of the mill strike days, when no one dared walk alone, and Tabby's lavish collection of Haworth crimes, scandals and murders. Richest of all were their own adult experiences, narrow but deep as the pit of hell itself. It was no task for their imaginations to supply the rest.

By their middle teens the girls had recognized that parsons' daughters had to be self-supporting and that the only refined work was teaching, so Charlotte and Emily went to Roe Head to prepare themselves with the idea of coaching Anne at home. Though this school was no Cowan Bridge, they were still lonely and miserable. However, Charlotte did find there a lifelong friend and confidante, Ellen Nussey. To this gentle girl she was to pour out her heart in innumerable letters over the years, and Ellen's visits were often her only contact with the outside world. Silent, withdrawn Emily on the other hand made no friends at all, and grew so sickly that Charlotte, in a panic, had her sister sent home.

Emily was an enigma to the family; incapable of life away from the moors, at Haworth she helped Tabby with the housework and took long solitary walks, serenely happy in a way she never explained except in her poems. Nevertheless, the tall, graceful girl with the haunting eyes that seldom met another's directly was the one the family loved best of all.

Unlike Emily, Charlotte was open, direct and positive. Depressed by her plainness, she absorbed education ravenously, for if governessing was to be her fate and Anne's, excellence must be their ambition.

Branwell's future was another matter. Boys could aspire to any career they chose, and he, who wrote, painted, played musical instruments, composed, and conversed like a god, was the genius and must have every opportunity. So while the shy, awkward girls trained for their profession, their idol cut a dash at the Black Bull tavern in the village, dazzling its patrons with his wit and, unknown to his father, acquiring a taste for rum.

For several years the Misses C. and A. Brontë taught in

various fine homes, Charlotte forever chafing at "the asinine stupidity of these little blockheads," while the more docile Anne adapted to the work somewhat better. Branwell meantime leaped from career to career, applied to the Royal Academy of Art and then failed to show up, wrote pretentious poems and novels that never came to anything. At each failure he retreated further from reality, turning to rum and laudanum to comfort himself. For a long time his family would not face the truth about him and life at the parsonage went on as unruffled as ever.

This parsonage, indeed, was a place of incredible monotony. Aunt Branwell and Mr. Brontë seldom left their rooms, while Tabby and the maid kept to the kitchen. The only callers were Mr. Brontë's curates and, for a short time, piano and drawing teachers. Otherwise all was silence. But underneath, hidden forces heaved and strained as epics in Byronic mood flowed from the children's pens, melodramas involving the grandiose Angrians and Gondalians. Sometimes they collaborated with one another and sometimes wrote separately, in secret. Once or twice Charlotte and Branwell, the ambitious ones, made an effort to secure publication, but in truth all were seeking not so much fame and money as relief from internal pressure. In a less restrictive environment these ardent spirits would have led the swashbuckling lives their natures craved; as it was, much of their creative force was driven awry—Charlotte's into the terrors of a nervous breakdown, Branwell's into debauchery, Emily's into mysticism, and Anne's into a melancholy piety.

Charlotte was twenty-three before the appalling monotony was breached. While Emily froze all men but her father and brother, and Anne never received any real attention, Charlotte had a certain vivacity—"the besetting sin of enthusiasm," she called it wryly—that was to attract more than one matrimony-bound man. Her first suitor had the virtue of being the brother of her dear friend Ellen Nussey. Nevertheless, she rejected the staid young curate out of hand. "You do not know me," she wrote him. "I am not the serious, grave, cool-headed individual you suppose. You would think me romantic and eccentric." And she explained her refusal to Ellen by saying, "I have not that intense attachment which would make me willing to die for him. If ever I marry, it must be in that light of adoration."

Her second suitor she dismissed even more abruptly. He was a young Irish clergyman brought to call, and she described him to Ellen as "witty, lively, ardent, but deficient in the dignity and discretion of an Englishman. At home, you know, I am never oppressed by that miserable embarrassment which torments me elsewhere. So I conversed easily and laughed at this Irishman's jests, excusing his faults because of the amusement his originality afforded, but cooling a little when he began to season his conversation with flattery. He went away and no more was thought about him. But a few days later I got a letter—a proposal of matrimony. I hope you are laughing heartily." These businesslike young curates were shopping for a plain, virtuous helpmeet and housekeeper, but Charlotte could not yet settle for such a counterfeit love.

Her life in other people's homes was galling her more every day, and she longed for the independence of a school owned by the Misses Brontë. Aunt Branwell had offered to advance a hundred pounds toward such a venture, but there was one serious drawback—their faulty French. Then, propitiously, another school friend wrote from Brussels describing the beauties of that city. At this glimpse of a world beyond Yorkshire, Charlotte's heart nearly burst. "Something swelled to my throat," she wrote to Ellen, "such a desire for wings, such a thirst to see, to know, to learn!" And she was swept away by a plan: six months in Brussels would be the making of a French accent for herself and Emily. They must go, oh, they *must!* So in February, 1842, Mr. Brontë took the quivering Charlotte and listless Emily to the Pensionnat Heger in Brussels. If Charlotte's heart had yearned for this day, it would have fainted had it foreseen the morrow.

The Pensionnat Heger was owned by Monsieur Heger, a brilliant and eccentric teacher, and Madame Heger, an attractive woman three years her husband's senior, who ran him, the hundred pupils, and the other teachers with tact, firmness, and an eye that missed nothing. The school occupied a seventeenth-century mansion where the girls slept in long dormitories with curtained-off beds.

The two stiff foreigners in their dowdy clothes struck the giggling Belgians as ludicrous and conceited; Charlotte and Emily in turn withdrew into a fortress of Englishness, from which they wrote home, "If the national character of the Belgians is that of these girls, it is cold, selfish, animal and inferior. They are mutinous and difficult for the teachers to manage, and their principles are rotten to the core. We avoid them." Moreover, everyone at the school was Catholic, and the Methodist Brontës, brought up to regard the Church of Rome with contempt, buried themselves in their studies in a corner.

The two brilliant minds delighted Monsieur, but he soon recognized Emily's as the finer and said of her, "She should have been a man, with her powerful reason and strong imperious will." He would have enjoyed cultivating it, but Emily refused to respond to him, yearning only for Haworth. Charlotte, on the other hand, responded more eagerly than she knew. Monsieur was the first true intellectual she had ever met, and the daily contact with his vibrant mind was electrifying. Her first letters to Ellen were deliberate efforts to make light of him: "He is a little black being; sometimes he looks like an insane tomcat, sometimes a delirious hyena. Occasionally he discards these perilous attractions and assumes an air almost mild and gentlemanlike." But presently she revealed more than she intended: "When he is very ferocious with me I cry, and that sets all straight."

Halfway through the school year, the blossoming idyl was shattered by news that Aunt Branwell was dying. Never the mother the girls needed, still, she had been fair and kind, and now, arriving home for the funeral, they learned that she had left her modest income to finance their school. Charlotte, ablaze with plans, saw events obligingly falling into place. Though Branwell was drinking more and working less, Anne's employers had accepted him as their son's tutor, which solved one problem. As to Mr. Brontë, he was developing cataracts and would be needing someone's care, but Emily did not wish to leave home again anyway, so she could perform that duty. Charlotte returned to Brussels with an easy mind, convinced that all was well.

Indeed it would have seemed so, for now Madame Heger offered her sixteen pounds to teach Monsieur and the girls English, while perfecting her own French. But without Emily she was lonely and lost, an English wren in a cage of Belgian macaws. Her only happiness was during Monsieur's lessons, when his efforts at pronunciation made a delightful excuse for laughter. Thirstily she drank of these exhilarating moments, but Madame began to notice her excitement and developed a certain chill. Monsieur still lent her books but now she saw him only at the lessons; then Madame's brother invited himself to join them. Finally the lessons ceased altogether. Charlotte in her innocence could not understand why.

Years before, after Emily had been sent home from Roe Head, Charlotte had been all but insane with loneliness, a prey to terrors she could not name. A perceptive doctor had saved her reason by returning her to her family, but now there was no such doctor around. And when the long August vacation arrived, sending the pupils home and the Hegers to the seashore, Charlotte was alone in the great house with one maid. In the cavernous silence she became hysterical, driven out to walk the streets by the hour until she returned to her bed exhausted, only to endure dreams worse than waking. In time her anguish brought on fevers and hallucinations, and sensing her own danger, she wrote to Branwell: "All alone in the great dormitory, I find myself returning fanatically to the old Angrian faces and scenes." Dwelling in these narcotic fantasies of knights and princesses and monsters she came perilously near madness, and the frightened maid tried to call a doctor. But Charlotte knew her only hope lay elsewhere.

Sometimes her walks had taken her past the Roman Catholic Cathedral of St. Gudule, when she would turn her head away and hurry on. But now in desperation she entered and crept into a confessional to pour out her agony. No one ever knew what she told the priest, for she mentioned the incident only casually to Emily, but the relief she gained sustained her for a few weeks longer. By October, however, the strain was again beyond sufferance and she gave notice. Madame was quick to accept it, but Monsieur blindly refused, and she hesitated, paralyzed by confusion. At last the release came through Mr. Brontë, who was nearly blind and needed her at home. This time Monsieur let her go, and they bade each other goodbye.

Again no one knows the words that were spoken, but in Charlotte's novel *Villette* there occur both a confession and a farewell scene that have the ring of real life. It would appear that Monsieur, while not professing love, had implied a very special friendship—enough to tinge the ordeal of departure with hope. "However long I live," she wrote Ellen, "I shall not forget what the parting cost me." This was the last time she ever mentioned his name, for once at home she realized the full force of her feelings. Then the real nightmare began.

The torturous facts came out only after her death, when four of her letters to Monsieur were published, letters revealing such hunger, such agony, such humble yearning, as to wring any reader's heart even a hundred years afterward. The correspondence began with brave composure as she told of her efforts to start a school, her father's failing eyesight, her own fear of blindness. Then she burst out, "I must see you. As soon as I have earned enough money I shall go to Brussels, and I shall see you again, if only for a moment."

None of his replies was ever found, but judging by her frantic appeals, he did his best to discourage the correspondence, even ignoring her first letter for a full six months. In mounting anguish as the months passed she wrote again: "Day and night I find neither rest nor peace. If I sleep I am tormented by dreams in which I see you, always severe, always grave. Forgive me, Monsieur, if I write you again. How can I endure life if I make no effort to ease its suffering?"

He must have ordered her not to write oftener than once in six months, for her next letter was even more desperate.

> Monsieur, the poor ask only for the crumbs that fall from the rich man's table. But if they are refused they die. Nor do I either need much affection from those I love. I should not know what to do with a friendship entire and complete, I am not used to it. But you showed me a *little* interest in Brussels, and I hold onto that as I would onto life.

This time he must have been even more obdurate, for it was nearly a year before she wrote again.

> Your last letter was nourishment for half a year. Now I need another, and you will give to me, not because you bear me friendship but because you are compassionate of soul. I have tried to forget you, I have denied myself the pleasure of speaking about you even to Emily, but when day by day I await a letter, and day by day nothing comes, fever claims me, I lose appetite and sleep. May I write you again next May? I would wait a year, but I cannot. It is too long.

He never answered this letter at all, and now she had to endure life totally without hope. Not until many years later, when she purged herself in *Villette*, was she free of her pain.

These were desolate days. Her eyes were giving her trouble; Mr. Brontë was ever more dependent, Emily ever more removed; and Branwell and Anne were away at the Robinsons'. She felt a hundred years old, though she was only twenty-eight. Still, this vivid spirit could not help yearning "to break a lance on the rough realities of life."

Branwell soon presented her with just such a rough reality. He had been drinking heavily for years, and one day he reeled in from the Robinsons' to pour out a tawdry tale. He and Mrs. Robinson, who was seventeen years his senior, had become lovers, and her husband had driven him out with threats to his life. The lady, he said, was as heartbroken as he and was only prevented from following him by powerful and wealthy interests.

This paranoia was to devastate his remaining years and make life at Haworth hideous. Rum and opium having taken over completely, he set fire to the bedroom he shared with his father and threatened both their lives. The family wearily accepted his stupors and rantings—Anne in shame and terror, Charlotte in disgust, Mr. Brontë with breaking heart. Only Emily retained enough affection to wait up nightly to put him to bed. The parsonage's future stretched bleakly to the grave.

Bleakly it would have ended, too, save for a merciful accident when, one afternoon in 1845, Emily forgot to close her little folding desk. Charlotte, coming in later, saw a notebook nearby and unthinkingly opened it and read it. In wild excitement she ran to find Emily. "I have read your poems!" she cried, embracing her. "They are magnificent, Emily! They stirred my heart like a trumpet."

Emily seized the notebook, indignant at the intrusion, but Charlotte stood her ground. "These are no ordinary women's verses. They are vigorous and genuine. They must be published," she insisted.

Emily stared incredulously, but Charlotte's enthusiasm at

last calmed her anger. They argued for days before Emily would even consider publication. Then Anne said to her "Since you like Emily's poems, Charlotte, you might care to look at mine."

Though Anne's were no match for Emily's, Charlotte was delighted, and now she too confessed to her share of verse. At this point her besetting sin of enthusiasm took over and she cried, "Why should we not publish them together?" Emily agreed providing they use pseudonyms. Each contributed twenty-one poems, and they sent them off. But no publisher showed any interest, so finally they decided to have them printed privately, using some of Aunt Branwell's money to underwrite the cost.

This action broke the miasma, for they next discovered that each had been working on a novel, Charlotte's about life in Brussels, Emily's about life on the moors and Anne's about the life of a governess. Saying nothing of their projects to Mr. Brontë, to Branwell, or the servants, they gathered with renewed verve each evening around the dining table and wrote.

Externally all was unchanged except for the unimportant fact that Mr. Brontë had a new curate, of whom Charlotte wrote Ellen, "Mr. Arthur Nicholls is from the north of Ireland and appears a respectable young man who I hope will give satisfaction. But I regard all curates as highly uninteresting specimens of the coarser sex." So much for Mr. Nicholls.

In May 1846, *Poems,* by Currer, Ellis and Acton Bell, appeared. One or two critics noticed Ellis's inner power, but only two copies were sold and the edition sank like a stone. Nonetheless, the novels were finished and sent into the world.

Mr. Brontë's cataracts being now ready for surgery, Charlotte took him to lodgings in Manchester and held his hand during the operation. Afterwards she resigned herself to sitting out the three weeks till he could travel again. All was silence in his shaded room; she had a toothache and her eyes smarted, but a new tale, dark and romantic, had taken possession of her thoughts. To pass the time she began to write about an orphan named Jane Eyre.

During the following months, while Charlotte dwelt with Jane in her thoughts, her earlier novel *The Professor*, Anne's *Agnes Gray* and Emily's *Wuthering Heights* were sent to publishers and came back monotonously. Everyone in the parsonage suffered from colds and bronchitis, Branwell continued to soak up rum, and the only news worth retailing to Ellen was the visit of a sheriff regarding Branwell's debts, a visit which did nothing to raise the general spirits.

At last a publisher offered to bring out *Agnes Gray* and *Wuthering Heights* if the authors would share the expense, and after some hesitation they agreed. Only Charlotte's manuscript caught no publisher's eye. Then, in 1847, her literary tide turned also. Messrs. Smith, Elder of London wrote that Mr. Currer Bell's manuscript, *The Professor*, showed such excellence of composition and discernment of character that while they could not undertake the present work they would be pleased to consider another from the same author. After a few days of frantic polishing such a manuscript went off.

Jane Eyre reflected many of Charlotte's experiences—the miserable child-years at Cowan Bridge, the moaning woman mysteriously secluded upstairs, the orphan desolation. There was, finally, the dream she wished for herself, the Cinderella ending. The manuscript went to Smith, Elder's first reader, who was at once impressed and so reported. Mr. Smith skeptically passed it to another reader, who was equally moved. Mr. Smith then took it home with him for the weekend. He had arranged to ride with a friend on Sunday morning, but having started to read at nine o'clock, he sent word at noon that he could not appear. When lunch was announced he called for a sandwich and read on. Dinner he gobbled hastily, finishing the manuscript before bedtime. Then far into the night his mind raced with publication plans.

Rushed out in six weeks, the book was a dramatic success, too sensational, some said, and a little naughty, but strangely fascinating nevertheless. A good portion of London started asking itself who this man Currer Bell might be, he who understood so well the feminine heart.

At Haworth no one suspected anything was afoot, for London letters came to *Mr. C. Bell, under cover to Miss Brontë,* and while Charlotte was banking Smith, Elder's payment of five hundred pounds she was writing calmly to Ellen: "We go on here much as usual—only Branwell more troublesome than ever. Mr. Nicholls returned from holiday. I cannot see any goodness in him; his narrowness of mind strikes me chiefly."

When the book's success was assured, Charlotte determined to break her silence and, shaking with excitement, took a copy and a few press clippings to her father. "Papa," she said, "I have been writing a book."

Without change of expression he looked up, vacant but kindly. "Have you, my dear?"

"Yes, and I want you to read it."

"Oh," he sighed, "I am afraid it will try my eyes too much."

"But it's not in manuscript, it's in print."

"Oh, my dear Charlotte," he said fretfully, "have you thought of the expense? It will surely be a loss. How can you get a book sold?"

"Papa, I don't think it will be a loss," she murmured and, after reading aloud a few of the reviews, left him with the book. At teatime he came into the drawing room.

"Girls," he said in wonder, "do you know Charlotte has been writing a book? And it is much better than I would have thought likely." In his bland self-absorption he did not even think the situation strange.

Shortly afterwards the other two novels were hurried out to take advantage of the Bell name. Anne's was generally ignored, but *Wuthering Heights* called forth active distaste: "It is a fiend of a book," one critic declared, and another: "It is hardly likely to find its way into a decent household." Even loyal Charlotte wondered whether it was quite right to create such creatures as Heathcliff, and later, after Emily's death, felt it necessary to explain her sister to the public. "She had no more practical knowledge of the world around her than has a nun," she wrote in a Preface to the second edition. "Except to go to church or walk on the moors she rarely left home. She could hear *of* people with interest, but *with* them she rarely exchanged a word. What she had heard was too often their tragic and terrible traits, and her imagination—more somber than sunny—found in them material for creations like Heathcliff, like Catherine. She herself did not know what she had done. If an occasional reader shuddered at these spirits so lost and fallen, if he complained that certain fearful scenes banished sleep by night, she was astonished and bewildered."

Though this fiend of a book was slow of acceptance, thirty years later critics were calling it a work of true genius, seeing in it, variously, Branwell's tortured love affair; an unconscious, unexpressed attachment between her brother and Emily; a conscious study of good and evil; even a hymn to love as a natural force becoming evil only when repressed.

The book's immediate effect was to take Charlotte and Anne to London. Its publisher had circulated the rumor that Currer, Ellis, and Acton Bell were one and the same person, and Smith, Elder asked Charlotte for clarification. Horrified, she declared they must all go at once and identify themselves. Emily flatly refused. "But you could see London at the same time!" cried Charlotte.

"Why should I?" said Emily. "You will bring it all back to me."

So the other two walked four miles to the railroad station in a thunderstorm and next morning, in London, went straight to the office of Mr. George Smith. A handsomely bearded young man received them civilly.

Charlotte, shaking and speechless, held out one of his letters. "Where did you get this?" he demanded in such bewilderment that she burst into laughter.

"I am Currer Bell," she said. "This is Acton. And Ellis Bell is at home. We are three sisters."

The next few days left the two in a state of collapse. There was a deluge of congratulations and questions, and then of invitations. Charlotte laughed to find Anne and herself at the opera with Smith and his two fashionable sisters. "We are not accustomed to this sort of thing," she whispered, and he pressed her arm in quick response. When they went home they took tales enough to last Emily for many weeks.

This pleasant interlude was shattered by Branwell, introducing a period of sheer horror. After the Robinson scandal he had persuaded himself that when the lady's elderly husband died he would marry her and share the Robinson fortune. However, when the old gentleman did oblige, word came that the widow was indeed going to remarry—not Branwell, unhappily, but a certain Sir George Scott. At the news Branwell let out a dreadful cry and fell on the floor in convulsions.

His weakened frame had already given way to tuberculosis, and now his mind failed too. There were maniacal scenes that left his family so stupefied that his death at last brought only relief.

The relief was but momentary. At the funeral Emily caught a chill; a few days later, at the memorial service, she began coughing, and later also developed tuberculosis. Charlotte did her best to nurse her sister, but this strange girl, so gentle yet harsh, so devoted to her family yet so estranged, rejected every overture, and her sisters were forced to let her die unaided.

Emily's nature is a fascinating study. A true mystic, she was nourished by satisfactions unknown to most human beings. Needing neither friends nor lover, she lived, as it were, within a private play of her own writing, among spirits of her own creation. She controlled every move of their lives, and apparently believed she had the same power over her own. Questioned about her condition, she only smiled; offered a doctor's help or medicine, she shook her head. Proudly, she refused even a supporting arm, and went about her duties defying weakness and pain. Charlotte, loving her more intensely every day, could only watch while she faded away, and within two months of Branwell's funeral Emily was dead.

Some feel that had Emily lived she would have lost her mind, some that she had already lost it. But there are others who declare that her poems reveal a sublime sanity comprehensible only by the very few and very fortunate.

To Charlotte, Emily had been "mine own bonnie love," and the emptiness she left seemed beyond endurance. But an even greater emptiness was brewing. Anne, the least brilliant of the four, had grown up in the imaginary Gondal with Emily, her softness supported by the other's strength. Now that strength was gone. Moreover, her second novel. *The Tenant of Wildfell Hall*, had been a failure. What she really yearned for most, marriage and motherhood, had been denied her, and lately she had drifted into a dispirited piety. Now, as Emily had fallen ill at Branwell's funeral, so did Anne at Emily's, and within six months she too was dead.

Charlotte's three dear ones gone in seven months, she staggered under the blow. And the vacuum of the next three years was even more terrible. She might have eased the loneliness in London, for her fame opened many doors, but her father needed her care and she found the stir of the city "a menace and a terror." Moreover, her experience with Monsieur had confirmed her most hopeless conviction regarding herself: "When a man looks at my face," she told a friend, "he never looks in my direction a second time." So she avoided all men, shielding herself from them behind a chilly disapproval.

Her work, however, introduced her to two whom she charmed in spite of herself. When James Taylor, a partner in Smith, Elder, displayed an interest at first professional and then personal, she nervously looked for defects in him and when nothing specific appeared she fell back on a general repugnance. Only after he had left for India did she let herself consider him, and then it was too late. She never saw him again.

Her relations with her handsome publisher were equally confused. He naturally made much of his prize author, but while escorting her about London he found himself sincerely charmed by her simplicity and zest. For her part, she felt a similar attraction that she controlled only by sternly reminding herself of her eight years' seniority. Nevertheless, their worlds were too foreign to permit any real conjoining and she retreated to Haworth and her desk with a kind of dismal relief.

Seven years had passed since the searing events in Brussels; she had touched on them gingerly in *The Professor*, but now she took hold with a sure grasp that made the resulting *Villette* one of her finest achievements. It went off to Smith, Elder and she sat down to wait—for what?

At thirty-six she had one companion, her father, the silent old man who appeared only at teatime, and one acquaintance, the curate who moved in and out of the house like a shadow. For eight years she had virtually ignored this "uninteresting specimen of the coarser sex," though Ellen Nussey liked him and even thought him handsome with his dark eyes and short beard. Then one day in December, 1852, the inconceivable happened.

Pouring tea according to routine for her father and Mr. Nicholls, she became conscious of a certain feverishness in the curate's glance, but after tea retired to the drawing room as usual. At nine she heard him in the hall bidding her father good night. Instead of going out, however, he tapped at her door and entered. In amazement she took in his deathly pallor and heard his half-strangled words. "Miss Brontë," may I speak? For months—for years—I know it is useless, but I must tell you anyway. . . ."

He loved her . . . humbly, with hopeless desperation. The sight of his trembling terrified her, and in confusion she stammered, "Have you spoken to my father?" He had not dared, and she cried out, "You must not speak to me, then." Embarrassed by his emotion, she half pushed him to the door and then rushed in to confess the whole thing to her father.

The old man was outraged; how dared this nonentity aspire to his famous daughter? More to the point, how dared he dream of depriving an old man of his last comfort and support? Later that night, still shaking, Charlotte poured out the story in a letter to Ellen.

> Papa was beside himself, furious. He worked himself up until the veins on his temples stood out and his eyes became bloodshot. My blood boiled, I confess, to hear the names he called the poor curate, but he was in no state to be trifled with and I made haste to promise that Mr. Nicholls should have a distinct refusal at once.

Still, she was torn by pity, and hearing that the poor man had refused food for three days, she wrote him a gentle letter: she could not marry him, of course, but he must be assured of her sympathy.

He was still beyond consolation. His miserable face depressed even the cook, and everyone left him completely to himself. At last he could endure it no longer and applied for another position.

On his last afternoon the parishioners gathered to present him with a gold watch. Mr. Brontë refused to attend the ceremony, and afterwards Charlotte, hiding across the hall, heard him go into the study to bid the old man goodbye. She wrote to Ellen:

> I thought it best to stay out of sight, but I could not forget his long grief, and when I heard him leave I took

courage and went out, trembling. I found him leaning against the front door sobbing as even a woman never sobs. I went straight to him. Very few words were exchanged, for he, poor fellow, wanted encouragement such as I could not give.

So Mr. Nicholls went away and a new curate took his place. But this man had the sort of faith that moves mountains. He wrote to Charlotte, begging for a word; dutifully she ignored the letter. After five more letters she replied. Submit to the inevitable, she pleaded; but there was that also in her letter which encouraged him to beg for another. The correspondence grew. After some months he asked her to meet him in a nearby village, and several such encounters took place, Charlotte always nervous and conscience-stricken. At last she summoned the courage to receive him at the parsonage.

Her father was still rude and sarcastic, but the new curate had proved unsatisfactory and he was feeling more in the mood to be won over. So the miracle happened. "The result of Mr. Nicholls' most recent visit, dear Ellen," she wrote, "is that Papa's respect is won and his consent gained, for he has in all things proved himself. I too respect Mr. Nicholls. In fact, dear Ellen, I am engaged."

The courtship that had lasted two years (ten, if the eight years of silent worship be counted) had been successful, and Charlotte, who had dreamed of Angrian passions, had settled for respect. "I trust to love my husband," she said. "I believe him to be affectionate, conscientious and high-principled. If I should regret that fine talents and congenial tastes are not added I should be most ungrateful." Soberly she prepared for the wedding, using her earnings to paper and paint the house, and to convert a small storeroom into a study for her husband. Her wedding outfit was white embroidered muslin with a green and white bonnet, and she was accompanied by Ellen and their Roe Head schoolmistress. When at the last minute Mr. Brontë refused to be present, Miss Wooler stepped in and gave the bride away.

The honeymoon took them to Nicholls' home in Ireland, where she was gratified to find a handsome house and a cultured family. "I was very much pleased," she confessed, "and greatly surprised. My dear husband appears in a new light here in his own country."

Indeed her life henceforth was one long surprise. She who had written to Monsieur Heger, "I should not know what to do with a friendship entire and complete," was receiving into her hands a daily tenderness, a fullness of devotion, that took her breath away. "How my life is changed!" she exulted, "To be wanted continually, to be constantly called for! It seems so strange."

Back at the parsonage, even her attentions to her father became more warm and spontaneous. "My wish for his happiness and health seems—I scarcely know why—stronger than before I was married." And finally the supreme miracle: this woman without pride in her womanhood, whom no man ever cared to look at twice, this woman was going to become a mother.

Some students of Charlotte Brontë have called her life unrelieved tragedy. Others, conceding her a moment of happiness, have doubted that Nicholls could have sustained the rapturous blaze he had lit and believe it would have had to sputter out. And he was, indeed, a questionable mate for a genius. Unable to understand her work, he was jealous and intolerant of it. Transformed by marriage into a typical Victorian family man, he expected his wife to ask his leave in everything. He even tried to supervise her correspondence with Ellen. This possessiveness might in time have destroyed their happiness. But there was not that much time; her star was still rising when it went out.

Branwell and four of his sisters had died of tuberculosis. Charlotte had been the hardiest, but even hers was a shaky structure. Married in June, 1854, she caught a severe cold that autumn. In the following March she died.

Nearing the end, she asked for a pencil and wrote a final note to Ellen: "My husband is the tenderest nurse, the kindest support, the best earthly comfort woman ever had." Her last words to Arthur were, ". . . we have been so happy." Surely this life cannot be called altogether a tragedy.

Jules Verne

(1828=1905)

Jules Verne

(1828=1905)

THE First World War brought forth a multitude of scientific inventions. The great French general, Hubert Lyautey, was telling his staff about a particularly advanced idea that had just been proposed, when one of his listeners smiled. "That sounds like something out of Jules Verne, sir."

"It does," the general replied. "But don't you realize, for twenty years all scientific progress has been something out of Jules Verne."

Verne once said, "Whatever one man can imagine, other men will some day bring to pass." And certainly, though there were no airplanes when Verne wrote about them, no electric lights, refrigerators, telephones, radio, television, automobiles, air conditioning, moving pictures, or bathyspheres, the things he imagined other men did in time bring to pass.

Jules Verne was born in the French city of Nantes near the mouth of the Loire. His parents were Pierre and Sophie Verne, descendants of shipbuilders, sailors and lawyers. From his mother he inherited the red streak in his hair, the fitful disposition, and the wildly roving imagination, while from his father came his logic and reasoning power. This good, upright lawyer was too strict for companionship with a small child (he kept a telescope eternally glued on a distant monastery clock, a slave to punctuality and his religion) and he tried to force his eldest son into his legal practice against his will. Nevertheless they eventually became fast friends and it was to him that Jules always turned in moral crises. The younger brother Paul was his other lifelong companion; these two were the extent of his intimates.

The Jules Verne of the future began to appear at seven when he wrote to an aunt, "Please come and visit us again, because I love you very much. And then, could you bring those little telegraphs you promised us?" The newly invented Morse keys were more exciting than tin soldiers to this little mind.

Also stimulating to it were the sailing vessels bringing back strange cargoes from far-off places, and the records of long-dead sea captains found in a warehouse. Everything of the sort went into his mental grab bag and came out later as material for his hundred-odd books.

So did his reading. As the eldest of five children he took his responsibilities solemnly, and to the group gathered around the hearth he would read aloud *The Swiss Family Robinson* and that other Robinson surnamed Crusoe. Later he recalled: "The Robinsons were *the* books of my childhood. My passion for their adventures put me on the path that I was going to follow." It is interesting to think how many other men were to say the same about *his* books.

Conscientious Father Verne also read aloud, mainly Walter Scott and Fenimore Cooper. These tales of long ago and far away, of physical conflict rather than of emotion, were to send Jules' mind spinning off to his own world of dreams and adventure and determine the whole course of his life.

To understand Verne's appeal as a writer one must understand his period. At the time of his birth France's way of life was breaking up painfully and re-forming in a new pattern. For centuries both England and France had been farming countries; but recently the factories and workshops of the Industrial Revolution had made cities the new centers, while railroads and steam engines were furthering the change.

JULES VERNE AT 25

The dislocation was intensified when the great scientist Charles Darwin challenged established beliefs with his theory of evolution, for then science became the new god and engineers and explorers the new priesthood. These upheavals left people feeling a little uneasy, many of them yearning for the former simple times and scenes. Hence the popularity of Scott and Cooper—and of Jules Verne. A desert island, the depths of the ocean, the other side of the moon, they were somewhere far removed from the disturbing realities of today.

This was the changing world Jules and the younger Paul entered at nine and eight when they left for boarding school. Jules hardly distinguished himself at the Lycée, dreaming more than he studied and filling his notebooks with ships and flying machines. He and Paul used to wander down to the shipyard to watch the steam "pyroscaphs" abuilding, and one day he said, "Paul, some day we'll buy a ship. Then we can make a trip around the world."

At eleven he tried to make this dream of adventure come true. Slipping out early one morning, he met a weeping boy at the town square who, it seemed, had been bound to a vessel just sailing for the Orient. "Cabin boy on a three-masted trading schooner!" This was how adventure stories began, and Jules quickly changed places with the boy and found himself aboard the *Coralie* sailing down to sea.

It happened that the *Coralie* had one last home call to make, and when she reached Paimboeuf that evening a tall stiff figure was waiting on the wharf. An excited neighbor of the Vernes had reported seeing Jules board the ship, and his father had overtaken the *Coralie* in a swifter boat.

Jules the adventurer was mortified, but Jules the little boy was weak with relief, for as the hours passed he had grown sicker and sicker. Meekly he accepted his beating, meekly ate his penitential bread and water, and to his tearful mother he made a promise: "I'll never travel again, except in my imagination." The strange thing is that, like so many of his most unlikely prophecies, this one came true. That single day away from home was the nearest he ever came to a real adventure.

His adolescence passed without unusual event. At high school he wrote madly—poems and morbid tragedies no one would take seriously. And of course he fell in love. But the beautiful Caroline Tronson was just his own age and therefore years older in worldly wisdom. He had always acted the clown in their childhood games and though by the age of nineteen he had developed into a romantic-looking youth with a fine profile and arresting red-gold hair—though he was witty and engagingly unpredictable—she still could only laugh at his lovemaking. When she announced her engagement to another, he fled to Paris, willing even to endure law examinations to escape witnessing the wedding.

When it was all over he wrote home, clowning again to hide his hurt.

> So she is really married! Well, I say simply, "Father, forgive her, for she knows not what she does." I'll take my revenge by killing her big white cat at the first opportunity.

Soon afterwards, to please his father and to forget Caroline, but mainly to be near the theatre world, Jules took permanent quarters in Paris. He was supposed to be studying law—and in off moments he did—but his best hours went into writing. He was going to be a great playwright.

His student days were typical in one way but not in another. True, he lived in a garret with a friend; true, they shared one suit of evening clothes and could go out only singly, and he lived once on dried prunes for three days to buy a set of Shakespeare. But there was a substantial and loving family at home who would always respond to a wail of hunger, and there were relatives in Paris who could introduce him to the wealthy, the chic and the clever.

Jules Verne

In no time he was mixing with minor celebrities—writers, artists and politicians. He joined a group, The Eleven Without Wives, who met once a week to dine modestly and talk extravagantly; he filled in at dinner and theatre parties. He even met Alexander Dumas, author of *The Three Musketeers.* This amazing man, famous father of a famous son, was one of the sights of Paris. He had built himself a castle, "Monte Cristo," with a stable, a monkey house, a theatre, an artificial lake and, on an island, an octagonal studio with the title of a play or book on each of its sides. Here he wrote, and here alone none of his guests was admitted. Otherwise these hordes came and went, eating and drinking from his limitless generosity. He helped young artists by the score and, among others, took the attractive youth from Nantes under his wing.

Since Dumas owned his own Paris theatre, Jules was privileged to watch rehearsals and share the star's box at openings. And when he diffidently brought out a few plays he had written, Dumas put on one of them, a slight bedroom farce. Thus he introduced him to his first career. Better, he inspired him to his second.

Dumas was author of a great series of historical novels. Jules, who was enamored of everything scientific and had decided that his dramatic trifles were a waste of time while science was pushing into the unknown, now outlined a tremendous series of scientific novels to parallel the other's. Dumas was enthusiastic. "Go ahead," he said.

"Do you really think I can do it?" Jules asked.

"Why not?" was the comforting reply, thus settling something wavering in the younger mind. At the moment, Jules needed all his resolution, for even with the production of his farce his writing had earned him not a single penny, and now that he had his law degree he was expected home in the law office. Thus he had to choose between disappointing his father's hopes and his own. After a struggle he chose to disappoint his father's.

"Dear Father," he wrote. "I have decided to remain in Paris and work at my writing. It is fate that keeps me here. I may become a good writer but I should certainly be a poor lawyer, for I only see the comic or artistic side of things. If I took over your practice it would simply wither away. Please forgive your respectful and loving son, Jules." Not unexpectedly, his father shut off his allowance, not so much to show anger as to discourage his son's hopeless course and bring him to his senses.

Now Jules was on his own, perhaps a little shaky but grimly determined. He wrote without letup—plays, stories and articles, working increasingly in the scientific field, and after hearing an explorer named Arago lecture on the Colorado gold fields and Brazilian jungles, dreams of far-off, unreachable places set his mind on fire. His study of geography became an obsession.

At this time Edgar Allan Poe was taking all France by storm with his *Tales of the Grotesque,* and Verne, embracing with delight this new writer's codes and ciphers, his ghoulish imagination and powers of analysis, found his own imagination somehow unleashed. "A Balloon Journey" combined aeronautics, geography, and the grotesque in a tale of a madman stowed away aboard a balloon, and though as art it was insignificant, as the first step in a new style it was a landmark.

But his money still ran from short to nonexistent, and Jules considered a couple of alternatives: law clerking, which he soon quit in disgust; then marriage, which was probably more practical, since French brides brought comfortable dowries with them. But he was saved from this extremity by Dumas, through whom he became secretary of the Lyric Theatre at 1,200 francs a year. Suddenly he was on easy street; he had a steady income, a part in the hypnotic world of the theatre, and leisure to write. Like a fountain unstopped he turned out cheap operettas and comedies for the Lyric and at the same time wrote experimental stories for himself.

Jules Verne

At home in Nantes the Vernes kept an embarrassed silence about these questionable activities. But Father Verne was wavering, for in Nantes he was known as "the lawyer with the soul of a poet," and once he had swallowed his disappointment he embraced the new situation with enthusiasm. Moreover, his doubts about his son's morals were relieved on reading a novel he had just written, in which was depicted the battle between the old religion and the new science. In it religion came out ahead. Thus all was well on that score, too.

"My son has a sort of extravagant genius," boasted the proud father, and he begged Jules to apply for a French Academy prize. Recognition from the Academy was the goal of all artists' ambitions, membership in it the guarantee of immortality, neglect by it the deepest stab to the heart. Secretly, Jules yearned for even the slightest nod from that direction, but he said proudly, "If I must bow and scrape to obtain the prize I would rather do without."

For nearly five years the Lyric secretary wrote worthless plays, prepared posters and settled singers' quarrels, but as the novelty of a steady salary wore off, so did the pleasure. Restless and exhausted, he began to lie sleepless the night through with an agonizing migraine paralyzing the left side of his face—the penalty of overwork that was to plague him the rest of his days.

A friend in Nantes, whither he had gone for a visit, noted his misery and said, "You look awful, Jules, jumpy and nervous and gray as an oyster. Why not give up that fast life in Paris and settle down here where you belong?"

Jules shook his head. "I have a thousand ideas to write and I need to be near the libraries. But," he admitted, "something is wrong with me."

"Maybe you should get married."

Jules looked thoughtful. "Have you any suggestions?"

"Well, there's to be a masked ball in a few days. With your

theatrical experience you should be able to make an impression on some young lady."

Jules went to considerable trouble to devise a special costume, and so dashing was he altogether that while one attractive girl of a wealthy family was plainly taken with him, her less susceptible father never let them out of his sight. Unfortunately Jules, whose tongue at times carried him away, made an overbold remark which the father happened to hear. This, combined with the father's knowledge of Jules' meager salary, did nothing for the young man's suit. He went back to Paris and his migraine, as solitary as before.

The turmoil of the theatre finally became intolerable, and breaking free, he threw himself full time—sixteen or eighteen hours a day—into the task of becoming a serious writer, perfecting his style and acquiring a comprehensive scientific vocabulary. Every thought, even an order to the laundry, had to be precisely expressed, every available fact of science pursued and nailed down.

This author of a hundred books was the victim of his own genius—"genius," that is, in the sense of "jinn" or indwelling spirit. His demonic imagination made him a world-famous figure; at the same time it enslaved him like a drug. He could not take a day's trip to the seashore without a plot wrapping itself about the incident, or lose a watch without being seized by a story. There was no stopping his spinning fancies, and in the belief that he had inherited this demon from his mother, he once chided her affectionately: "This imagination of yours! It moves faster than a locomotive, faster than an electric spark, faster than a tropical waterspout. It gives me no peace."

Like most writers, he required solitude, and, also like them, he was crazed by the loneliness. His worried parents searched for a suitable wife for him, but not one possibility got beyond the discussion stage. Then all of a sudden his demon seemed to relent. He had gone to Amiens to see a friend married, and there he met the sister of the bride. "Imagine, dear Maman," he wrote a week later, "I believe I have fallen in love! She is a young widow of twenty-six with two little girls. Oh, why does she have to have two children? I always run up against impossibilities."

Honorine de Viane Morel was a tall handsome girl, laughing and cheerful, and she accepted him at once. The real "impossibility" was the state of his own finances, for while poverty in an artistic young bachelor was one thing, to a man contemplating marriage it was something else. But Honorine's brother had given him an idea. "Young de Viane," he wrote his father, "makes 50,000 francs a year as a stockbroker in Amiens. In Paris I could do even better, and should need only two or three hours a day at the Exchange. Could you possibly advance me the price of a share in a broker's business?"

Poor Father Verne had just begun to enjoy having a writing son, and he replied, wistfully, "One more illusion gone! Instead of being a writer, my son is to become a stock-jobber!"

Jules responded with an appealing simplicity that ended the father's argument: "I am tired of living alone. I am twenty-nine and my heart is desperately empty. This may strike you as comical, coming from me, but I just want to be happy." So he got a share in a broker's office and married his Honorine in January, 1857.

No apartment being available till October, the bride's mother took the two little girls and Honorine moved to Jules' one-room flat. Singing and laughing, he carried her furniture up the five flights on his back, and four days after the wedding he took her to see the Venus de Milo. "There, my dear," he said, with unusual softness, "let me introduce you to the only woman you need ever feel jealous of."

For the next six years he lived a double life: rising at five, he half dressed, swallowed a cup of coffee, and read, made notes and wrote till ten. His desk had two drawers, one for science, the other for fiction, and he worked from them alternately. At ten he ate breakfast, donned a sober business suit and went to the Exchange where, between occasional trades, he bantered with a group of kindred wits. "He was the best among us," one of them recalled later. "He had a heart of gold, though he seldom let anyone see it." Others found less warmth: "He was tempered steel. He bent for his friends, but remained stiff for others. It was his voice, I think, quick and imperious, that made him seem so curt." Already he was developing that invisible shell which, despite his boyishly curling hair and handsome features, made him so forbidding in maturity.

After three years on the Exchange, he and his brother Paul secured a steamship pass for a trip to Scotland, then on to Liverpool, where they saw a transatlantic liner on the ways. Back at home he said to Honorine, "The moment I saw the *Great Eastern* I swore I would cross the Atlantic in her as soon as I had made a literary success."

She looked at him gently; they had been married three years and there were no signs of that success yet. "Are you quite sure you will, dear?"

"Unshakably," he replied stoutly. But to his father he wrote: "Sometimes I feel so depressed I can hardly go on. I'm still convinced I shall reach my goal, but I am already thirty-two. And I used to think that by thirty-five I would have an assured place in literature."

Success by thirty-five. Had he, had his father and Honorine, known his accuracy of forecast, they would have rested easier. And Honorine might not have written so anxiously to her mother-in-law: "Jules is finishing a story about balloons—always balloons. There are manuscripts everywhere, nothing but manuscripts. Let's hope they don't finish up under the cooking pot." At times they did go into the stove.

In 1861 their son was born, and now more than ever Honorine needed all the patience she could muster. Although Jules was ecstatic at first, he was not fully prepared to be a father and he soon began to retreat to his science club for peace. The following year he was still writing his long-suffering father: "The moment I get an idea, it goes wrong. If I write a play for a particular director, he moves away; if I write an article, another appears on the same subject. I do believe, if I discovered a new planet, it would explode just to prove me wrong."

But he was nearing thirty-five; his day was coming.

The first visit he had paid at the office of the publisher, Hetzel, had been futile. But now suddenly things were different. Hetzel, a creative artist, was starting a magazine for young people and had recently launched a series of books for young readers. An individualist who worked late and slept late in a room next to his shop, he had covered its walls, ceiling and doors with Flemish tapestries depicting medieval life. When Jules knocked and entered, he saw a form with long hair and lean aristocratic face lying in a medieval bed.

"Well, what is it?" Hetzel asked.

Advancing silently, Jules laid a manuscript on the table. "I have written a book about Africa . . . and a balloon trip."

Africa was very much in the news at the time, for Livingstone had opened up vast new territories and Speke, Grant and Burton were making spectacular stabs at the sources of the Nile. Balloons were likewise much discussed. "Leave it," said Hetzel. "Come back in a fortnight."

On returning two weeks later, Jules was braced for the usual disappointment. When Hetzel began, "I'm very sorry to tell you—" he reached for the manuscript. "—that in spite of the merit of the work—" the writer had started for the door.

"Wait!"

Verne stopped without turning. "I want to tell you," Hetzel went on, "that I can't use this manuscript exactly as it is. But you are a great storyteller, and if you will make some changes and then let me see it again . . ."

Jules was scarcely able to breathe. "Tell me what you mean," he said.

In a few skillful sentences, Hetzel dissected the manuscript and put the pieces back together, reshaped and redistributed, while Jules listened, eyes glowing with excitement. This was an architect of ideas; this was a mind to play to!

Hugging his manuscript, he rushed home, kissed Honorine hastily, and flung himself at his desk, that desk with its separate compartments of fiction and science. Under this publisher's guiding hand, he might harmonize the two.

Within fourteen days he had reshaped his story into a well-constructed book and Hetzel, reading *Five Weeks in a Balloon*, knew he had found a major talent, a mind teeming with ideas and knowledge yet disciplined by logic. He promised immediate publication and asked the author for further ideas.

In amazement he listened to the program Jules had outlined to Dumas years ago. It would take much time to achieve, but without hesitation Hetzel drew up one of the most prodigious contracts ever signed by a writer—two books a year for the next twenty years, at 10,000 francs a book. Five times over the years he was to tear up the contract for a better one.

For Verne this was like bounding at one leap from a pit to a mountain peak. Drunk with joy, he paid one last glorious visit to the Exchange, and gathering his cronies about him, said: "Well, friends, I'm leaving you. I have written a novel in a brand-new form, and if it succeeds I shall have stumbled upon a gold mine. *Au revoir.*"

His was no exaggeration, for he had hit a gold mine. *Five Weeks in a Balloon* was an instant success, translated into every language of Europe and followed by a series of *Extraordinary Journeys* that kept appearing long past the contracted twenty years and made his name known around the world. If before he had poured forth ideas like an oil well, he was now an unquenchable gusher, and Hetzel started a journal of education and recreation in order to drain off the writer's vast output in weekly installments.

Although Verne explored all the sciences, geography was his favorite, being at the same time both concrete and far-reaching. He had once been shocked to hear an army general declare that Lake Tanganyika must be in Poland "because all Polish names ended in *ki* or *ka*," and with a reformer's zeal he set out to remedy such ignorance, studying every scientific publication he could find and interviewing every available explorer.

It is unclear what kept this man who lived by travel and adventure from ever seeking those things for himself, but it was probably the same thing that kept him from ever truly joining the human race. No one could get very close to Jules Verne, and as he achieved the satisfaction of public success his family and friends receded into the background of his mind. This disinterest in people would account for the wood-enness of his characters. He had early discovered a story formula that required three human figures, all male—one for intellectual action, one for physical, one for comic relief—and as few women as possible. Starting with *Five Weeks in a Balloon*, this cast reappeared over and over.

This lack of interest in people also accounts for his stilted dialogue, for such incredible utterances as those he gave to a man being charged by wild elephants: "Alas! we have no firearms. No human being may with safety dare the anger of these monstrous beasts."

None of these things mattered. Verne had a genius for taking the facts of prehistoric times and advancing them to the present, then like a mariner charting his course, drawing a line between the two and projecting it to infinity. Thus he achieved those remarkable forecasts that scientists and inventors have been catching up with ever since.

Although Jules Verne was forever withdrawing further

into his own interior world, his prosperity had a few external effects. Honorine was now wearing fashionable dresses and he himself had a new tailored look and confidence of manner; they lived in an imposing apartment and gave lavish parties, all of which somewhat compensated Honorine for other marital deficiencies. But the creator of this prosperity did not always add to the parties' gaiety. Sometimes Jules was kept away from them by his agonizing headaches; to others he came, but then he growled and insulted the guests, or else, with hyperthyroid abandon, indulged in practical jokes and bawdy remarks. No one ever knew what mood to expect of him.

The one thing constant was his writing, which never stopped for more than a few hours. Behind closed doors he would race through a story in pencil, then rewrite it more carefully in ink. And this was only the beginning, for he corrected proofs endlessly, returning them for a fresh printing six or seven times. Nothing but tremendous sales would have compensated his publisher for such expense, but it was the writer's care about detail that won him the respect of adults as well as children. The scholarly *Journal des Débats* serialized his next two books, *Journey to the Center of the Earth* and *From the Earth to the Moon,* before they came out as boys' books, and eminent scientists began to wonder about the possibility of such fantastic notions as the discovery of the North Pole or a rocket trip to the moon. (One of Verne's most extraordinary forecasts concerned the launching site of a moon rocket: after a squabble between the states of Texas and Florida for the honor of providing the launch center, his hero sets off in a rocket from a pad in Florida. This story was written in 1865!)

Verne, of course, could not know how near some of his inventions were to come, but he was savagely resentful of any criticism of his scientific accuracy, and out of sheer pride devoted eight years to a voluminous history of exploration, from the earliest times to the nineteenth century.

All this labor was wearing him down; he needed sea air and more seclusion than Paris afforded, and at last he found a fishing village to his satisfaction at the mouth of the Somme. Honorine was not charmed by the solitude of the place and their tiny cottage, but as she commented, "Jules always does exactly as he likes," so to Crotoy they went. Life was monotonous, but that was what he liked; the emptier the surroundings, he said, the more room for his thoughts and visions.

It was there, too, that the writer found something he could genuinely love. Though the *Saint-Michel* was a mere fishing smack, on her deck he spent happy hours sailing the English Channel. There he found relief from the cruel migraine, about which he said, "The sea wind cures the neuralgia that the wind of inspiration throws in my face."

There too he found escape from domestic ties. "Jules has left me again," Honorine complained to her aunt. "He has taken it into his head to go to Paris in the *Saint-Michel*. With the drought we are having, he will run aground on a sand bank. Still, that's his lookout. It will be a lesson to him, for he simply can't stay still for a moment." Marriage to a genius can have its drawbacks.

On the *Saint-Michel*, lying on his stomach within a few feet of the water, he wrote *Twenty Thousand Leagues Under the Sea*, about Captain Nemo and his *Nautilus*, that marvelous submarine run by electricity that had every comfort, including a pipe organ. Aboard it were the usual three male characters, while women this time were reduced to a mere memory of Nemo's lost love. The dialogue was as stilted as ever. Nevertheless, Nemo was such a sensation that though Verne killed him off at the end of the book, later he was forced to bring him back by popular demand.

In July, 1870, the bitter Franco-Prussian War broke out, and Verne and his *Saint-Michel* were conscripted for the coast guard, while Honorine took the children back to Amiens. He was emotionally untouched by the war and kept on piling up manuscripts. Then one day, after the war was over, he saw an advertisement in a Paris window, a leaflet for Cook's Tours which announced excitedly that thanks to modern high-speed transportation, a traveler could now go entirely around the world in three months. "Ninety days!" That was all his eager brain needed, and before he was back at his apartment Phileas Fogg and Passepartout were half-way into life.

Around the World in Eighty Days was serialized in a newspaper in 1872, and from the first issue the paper's circulation soared. People placed bets on Fogg's race with time; United States papers carried bulletins on its progress; and as the last leg across the Atlantic approached, two steamship companies tried to bribe Verne into bringing Fogg home on their lines.

This success was only the beginning for the novel. A stage presentation complete with a live elephant ran for two years, and (one of the few predictions he failed to make) the story was again a huge success ninety years later in moving pictures—a medium he did predict. Verne took little credit. "It isn't me or Phileas Fogg," he laughed. "All hail to the elephant."

But fame and the work that seemed to have him by the throat were becoming unbearably restricting. "Oh," he cried to Paul Verne, "to be free, free, free! Oh, to go far away on some tremendous adventure!" Hetzel and Paul tried to help him, but he was too old and his habits too fixed. The nearest he came to his own Extraordinary Journeys was an occasional cruise on his sumptuous yacht *Saint-Michel III*, and the nearest to an adventure was an encounter with invisible Arabs. While he and his son were cruising off the North African coast a storm drove them into a deserted bay. Warlike Arabs were reported to be hiding behind the sand dunes, and in an ecstasy of excitement the eminent author executed a war dance on the beach. His son fired a rifle into the air and the

Arabs replied in kind. But they never showed up, and that was all there was to the adventure, his best, his only.

Verne, now in his late fifties, was the idol of the public and the recipient of many decorations, including the Legion of Honor. There was even talk of election to the French Academy. It had not happened yet, but there was still time; that glorious crown rarely materialized till late in one's life.

Finally he did have an adventure, but it was something he would scarcely have chosen. His beloved brother Paul's son, Gaston, a boy with a seemingly brilliant future, had some time before suffered a mental breakdown and been confined to his home. One day in March, 1886, he escaped, wandered about aimlessly with a loaded revolver in his pocket, and then, on a wild impulse, rushed to his uncle's house. Verne, returning from his club at twilight, was just unlocking the front door when Gaston charged, waving the pistol. Verne grabbed the boy's hand and tried to twist it free, but two shots went off, one going into the doorstep and the other into the writer's leg below the knee. Then he fainted.

When he came to, Honorine was sitting beside the bed moaning: "Poor Gaston, his mind is gone. He keeps mumbling, 'I did it for Uncle Jules. Now he'll be recognized, now he'll be made a member of the Academy.' "

The wound was relatively slight, though of course painful and unnerving, but the damage it did was disproportionately great. Broken, apparently, by the fact that it was Paul's son who had doomed him to walk with a cane forever, he lay staring at the wall hour upon hour or endlessly composing cross-word puzzles to ease his restless brain.

On top of this blow came a succession of others: Hetzel, the man who had made his career, died, and then Verne's mother. Her death, following his father's some years before, ended that happy phase of life, even in memory. Finally he lost the *Saint-Michel IV*, the last in a line of boats all named the same.

This one was a trim steam yacht, and he yearned to take her wheel again—yearned to and at the same time feared to, for the question continually nagged at him—could he still take the gales with this unsteady leg? And the answer came all too soon when, steering her out to open ocean, he staggered with her first lurch and went sprawling to his knees.

No longer captain of his ship, he would not be mere cargo, with someone else at the wheel, and he sold the *Saint-Michel*. With her went what he loved best in life.

But not life itself, for he still had nearly twenty years to live. His son and the two girls were married by now, and he and Honorine left Paris and settled in Amiens. There he became town councilor and, among many civic activities, supervised the local theatre as well as its people. All the while he wrote steadily, with imagination as keen as ever. In 1889 he described a future city in the United States as having tall skyscrapers with airplanes hovering overhead, escalator sidewalks, telephones, television, advertisements projected onto the clouds, news transmitted instantaneously by picture and sound, and solar heating.

He received tokens of admiration from all over the world, and had he chosen he could have had many friends and a full life. Nevertheless, he was profoundly unhappy. Away from home he made a show of amiability, but inside all was bleak silence. Paul Verne became alarmed and begged him to go away for a while to take a fresh view. His nephews, who were shipowners at Nantes and were launching a new vessel named the *Jules Verne*, had invited him to be guest of honor. He accepted, but when the time came he was not there. Even to Paul he could only write:

> I was very sorry to miss the ceremony. But I am weighed down by too many sorrows to join in the family rejoicings at Nantes. All forms of gaiety have become unbearable, my character has profoundly changed, and I shall never recover from the blows that fate has dealt me.

What blows? The shooting accident and the family deaths were years earlier; it could not have been their doing. No one has ever known the answer. But Verne students have picked up a few hints.

It might have been the French Academy. He had always hoped to be considered a serious artist, and Academy membership would have marked him officially as one of the "Immortals." But it never came. "I have never taken my place in the literature of France," he mourned.

But even this was no sudden, sharp blow. It must have been something closer, more immediate. Verne was the least autobiographical of authors, but one of his last books may hold the key. *The Castle in the Carpathians* is different from his others, a brooding, romantic story about an exquisitely beautiful young opera singer, Stella, and a man obsessed by her memory.

The man has invented a remarkable instrument which he places in his opera box while she is singing. When the young singer suddenly dies he takes the instrument to his castle. There he sits with it nightly, a lover mourning his dead love, watching a screen on which appears her moving, singing image.

Here Verne may have hinted at some personal heartbreak. If so, no particulars are known, her name, her history, whether that final blow was indeed her death. He simply went on living with Honorine in silence and writing, writing, writing. Finally his eyes failed, then his health, and early in 1905 he died.

But the seeds he had sown bore abundant fruit. Marconi, father of radio, said seventeen years later: "Jules Verne made people see visions, wish they could do things, and stimulated them to do them."

William Beebe, exploring the ocean depths in his bathysphere, credited *Twenty Thousand Leagues Under the Sea* with inspiring him to see what really was down there.

Admiral Richard Byrd, flying over the South Pole, said: "It is Jules Verne who guides me here." Many of the men now pushing out into space have said the same sort of thing.

Verne was a man with a strange and unique gift, and though the Academy never made him an "Immortal," his followers all over the world have taken care of that.

Mark Twain

(1835=1910)

Mark Twain

(1835=1910)

FEW writers have revealed themselves more thoroughly in their books than did Mark Twain. He was Tom Sawyer in the flesh, and in meeting Tom one meets the Twain who was the very symbol of good-natured laughter.

There was another creature inside the same skin, however, a creature of terror and despair and loathing, and the whole life of the man was a tug-of-war between these natures. Two things only were fixed and unshaken: his humor, which brightened even the blackest moment, and his love for his wife, Livy, which lasted from the day of their meeting until his death.

Mark Twain was born Samuel Clemens, in 1835. His father, Judge John Clemens, a Kentuckian of unblemished honesty and no business sense whatever, had some years before bought a hundred thousand acres of Tennessee mountain land for four hundred dollars. Anybody but the judge might have turned a small profit on such an investment, but no Clemens ever made a cent in business and the mountains remained a tantalizing extravagance until Sam later in life wrote a book and a play about them and cleared a hundred thousand dollars—exactly a dollar an acre, which would have appealed to the judge's orderly mind.

In the 1830's the Middle West was an inviting land of opportunity, and the judge, having failed in Tennessee, took his wife to Florida, Missouri, population 100, where they increased the total to 108 with the aid of Orion, Pamela, Margaret, Benjamin, Samuel and Henry. Always hopeful and always misguided, the judge tried to run a store there and failed, then moved to Hannibal, and failed there. He placed his trust in a friend who cheated him out of every cent, and, just when his personal integrity had won him a court clerk-ship and something to eat seemed likely again, he developed pleurisy and died. Thereafter his widow and children picked up pennies as they could.

The family's poverty notwithstanding, Sam always thought of his childhood with affection, and his books are peopled with the friends of those days. Tom Sawyer's Aunt Polly was a picture of Sam's mother, and Tom's friend Becky Thatcher was a little girl named Annie Laurie Hawkins. ("I fell in love with Annie Laurie," he said later. "I had an apple and I gave her the core.") Injun Joe was the town of Hannibal's half-breed, and Huck Finn was really Tom Blankenship, the un-washed son of the local drunk. All the other boys had to take a bath occasionally, but not Tom Blankenship, a glorious free spirit who was the most envied boy in Hannibal.

Much of Sam's childhood was spent on a big farm belong-ing to his uncle, and here he made one of the important friendships of his life. He and Uncle Dan'l, a tall black slave, put their heads together over the problems of the world and Sam learned much of wisdom and loyalty from this man whom he described so lovingly in *Huckleberry Finn* as Jim.

All these people contributed to the brightness of Sam Clemens' character. At the same time, a measure of darkness was going into it, for Sundays and the hours spent in church were for him a foretaste of hell. Hymns were long and mournful; prayers dwelt gloomily on souls lost in sin, all, he felt, obviously aimed at himself; sermons were guided tours through the torments in store for him, and God, like a huge policeman, was waiting overhead to pounce at any moment. There was really no escape.

MARK TWAIN
(age ca. 34-35)

Sam, knowing he was doomed, tossed and screamed in nightmares each Sunday night, but each Monday morning he was back at his sinning ways; and so he went, piling up a reserve of guilt and fear that was to last the rest of his life.

His natural affinity for trouble extended to that of others, and before he was fourteen he had shared in a whole catalogue of dramatic experiences: he stumbled over a corpse in his father's office, where it had been carried after a fight; he saw a man shot in the public square, watched a slave beaten to death and a stranger stabbed. He was present when a drunkard was shot by a woman in self-defense, and he saw two of his playmates drowned. Worst of all, he killed a man himself—or so he thought.

On that occasion a drunken tramp had been locked in the town's one-room jail, and when Sam and his friend Tom Blankenship went for a look at him, the man called through the bars, "Hey, lads, give me a light for my pipe."

Although Sam knew that consorting with criminals was forbidden, he readily passed in a couple of matches before he and Tom went on their way. Later a red glow lit up the sky and, rushing back, they found the jail a blazing bonfire with the screaming wretch tearing at his bars. By now no one could get near him, and Sam watched in horror while the jail burned to the ground.

It was all his fault, everything always was. When his father died, that too was his doing, somehow. Even when his brother Ben had died years before, God, he was sure, had been striking at him through Ben, punishing Ben for Sam's sins. Always, to the end of his life, that huge merciless Policeman glowered overhead.

With all this melodrama in his daily life, Sam felt no need for education and fought it off like a disease. He might, indeed, have remained an ignoramus always except for one of those unaccountable incidents that characterized his career. Once, as he was walking down the street, a piece of paper was blown against his leg. Removing it, he saw that it was a page from a book—something about a girl named Joan of Arc who, it seemed, had been ordered by angels to lead an army in battle. Incredulous, he rushed home to learn more about her, and what he heard made him gasp with excitement. He devoured every book in the library about Joan, then about the France she had defended and the England she had defeated. Thus introduced to history, he moved on to other subjects and was soon packing his head with a miscellany of useful information.

In the meantime his brother Orion, as head of the family, had gone to St. Louis to work as a journeyman printer. Soon thereafter Sam spent a year with the Hannibal *Courier* as one of three printer's apprentices, entering the newspaper world, so to speak, by the back door. It was a dreary year for the three apprentices, who were promised board, lodging and two suits of clothes in lieu of wages; the second suit was never seen and the first turned out to be a castoff of the employer, who was extremely fat. They slept on the office floor and ate in the kitchen, later graduating to the dining room but always still so hungry they had to fill in with stolen potatoes at midnight.

After a year Sam and Orion left their jobs and began a series of foolish ventures. Orion bought a small Hannibal newspaper with borrowed money and took Sam on at $3.50 a week, which would have been fair enough could he have paid it, but after a year of working for nothing Sam lost interest and drifted to St. Louis, on to New York, and back to Orion for two more payless years. Finally, in Keokuk, Iowa, his life's course was settled by just such an accident as the one that had saved him from illiteracy.

He was strolling down Keokuk's main street when a bit of paper was blown against the wall. "Something about the look of it," he recounted later, "attracted my attention, and I gathered it in. It was a fifty-dollar bill, the largest assemblage of money I had ever seen in one spot. I advertised it in the papers and then suffered a thousand dollars' worth of distress lest the owner see the advertisement. Four days went by in this misery; then I felt I must take that money out of danger, so I bought a ticket to Cincinnati."

There the sight of the Ohio River reawakened a boyhood ambition. A riverboat pilot, he knew, drew a princely salary, and the moment the ship left shore the pilot was sole boss of vessel, cargo and passengers, not even the captain being permitted to question his authority. Sam yearned for such grandeur, so he bought passage on a New Orleans boat, the *Paul Jones*, and put his charm to work on its pilot.

The Clemens charm was a formidable weapon. One's attention was caught first by Sam's thatch of wild red hair and humorous brows, while the flat Missouri drawl rendered even the most commonplace remark somehow arresting. He was determined that Pilot Horace Bixby should teach him his craft, and during the three days' sail to New Orleans his tales of his own boating exploits, all of them amusing, some of them true, won him an arrangement requiring of him strict obedience, a down payment of a hundred dollars and four hundred more out of future earnings.

"It's a man's job," said Mr. Bixby. "You've not only got to learn how to handle a boat, you've got to learn the river by heart, every foot of the twelve hundred miles from St. Louis to New Orleans." Two years it took Sam, but he did it. He memorized every twist and bend, every deep and shallow, and the exact depth of each. He memorized the hidden rocks underwater, the plantations along the shore, and the hills and valleys behind them and the name of each. He learned the way they looked as he steamed downstream, and the entirely different way they looked going up. Then he found that the shoreline and the bottom were constantly changing, and that as fast as he memorized something about them he had to forget it and learn anew.

Sam's ear became accustomed to the drone of the lead-man's voice as he sounded the depths—"Mark six, mark four, mark twain, quarter twain"—and subconsciously he noted every change as one notes the striking of a clock. Finally, having acquired mastery of the ship in every weather and at any time of day, he was granted his license. He was a pilot, at $250 a month.

Thus began a period of grandeur he seldom reached again, for not only could he help Orion and his mother, but in his satin waistcoat, kid gloves and top hat he felt himself little less than a god. "I got so used to throwing orders around," he confessed later, "it hurt me all the rest of my life to say please."

It was a soul-satisfying existence, the pleasantest of all the professions he ever tried, which included grocery clerk, law student, blacksmith, bookseller, drugstone clerk, printer, private secretary, silver-mill operator, reporter, foreign correspondent, lecturer, author; and he would have remained with it had not the Civil War halted all traffic on the Mississippi.

Stranded again, he went back to work for Orion on a three months' venture that lasted seven years and brought new privations, dangers, hopes and disappointments. Orion, like his father always honorable and impractical, had been appointed Secretary of Nevada Territory, and Sam went along as his secretary, paying his own $300 stagecoach fare since Orion's sole wealth was four pounds of lawbooks and a huge dictionary.

At Carson City, Sam at once became a proper Westerner, swaggering about in a slouch hat, rough wool shirt and pants stuffed into top boots, and as there was nothing to do in Orion's office, he and another man put in a claim for three hundred acres of forest land. For three weeks they were timber ranchers, but unfortunately their campfire set the whole tract ablaze. They then went on to bigger things—silver.

This part of Nevada was one vast silver mine, and Sam, being a Clemens, naturally lost his head over it. He, with two lawyers and a blacksmith, all equally green, formed a digging party that turned up some shiny stuff which unhappily proved to be mica. Next he teamed with a real miner named Calvin Higbie, and they actually found silver. The vein was rich enough to make them both millionaires, and it seemed that even Sam Clemens could not avoid getting rich this time; but geniuses are different from other people, and he managed it.

The two rushed to town and recorded their claim, duly noting the clause requiring them to start work within ten days. That night neither of them slept. "I'm going to build a mansion in San Francisco," said Sam dreamily.

"Me too," said Higbie. "Brick. Three stories high."

"I'm going to Europe in the spring," said Sam. "Italy, Greece, Persia, Greece."

"I'll go along," said Higbie.

"We'll cut a dash," said Sam. "Like two eastern potentates. I'll never wear the same shirt twice."

"Me neither," said Higbie, and they both went to sleep.

The following day Sam learned that a friend of Orion's was ill and needed help. Before riding off he left a note in the cabin for his partner: *Higbie: have gone to nurse Nye. Be sure to start work within ten days.*

Ten days later he returned, having passed their mine on the way where he noticed an excited crowd milling about. In the cabin he found Higbie seemingly ready to cut his own throat, for he had missed Sam's note and, expecting Sam to start work, had gone off on a trip of his own. The ten-day period was up and a crowd was already staking out fresh claims at the mine site. And so it went.

The pattern of Sam's life was beginning to emerge, a pattern of chasing money by the business road while it was chasing him by another. Witness the next move. For some time he had been writing letters to the Virginia City *Enterprise* as a way of amusing himself, and to his surprise they were printed. "The *Enterprise* must be starving for news, to print such rubbish," he observed, "or else the editor is an idiot." Then the idiot asked him for "rubbish" on a weekly basis, and in consideration of the twenty-five dollars Sam became city editor.

Pseudonyms were fashionable at this time, and in memory of his riverboat days he took to signing his accounts of horse races, pumpkin shows and murders with the boatman's phrase Mark Twain, signifying "twelve feet," or "safe going." Later the story of "The Jumping Frog," which was published locally first and then republished all over the world, brought the name Mark Twain to national attention. Work on several different papers followed and success began catching up with him, willy-nilly.

His first important assignment for a prominent newspaper was a series on Hawaii, a place then as remote to Americans as the South Pole, where he spent five months and closed the visit with a sensational scoop. A small boat had landed there, having in it eleven nearly dead men who had left a burning ship forty-three days before and drifted four thousand miles, suffering indescribable tortures from thirst and exposure. The story had suspense, tragedy and triumph, and Mark, seriously ill himself at the time, was carried on a stretcher to their bedsides. His interview brought him national acclaim.

Here was one career well started. But Mark Twain's road was like a railroad track, two separate lines running parallel; for back in San Francisco he was asked to give a talk on the Islands, and though he laughed at the idea, an enthusiastic friend hired the opera house and he was forced to follow through. Together they wrote out an announcement that ended, *The doors open at seven o'clock. The trouble starts at eight,* and people who had laughed at "The Jumping Frog" began laughing again when they read it. That night as the terrified young man was pushed out onto the stage, a packed house burst into applause, and shout followed shout all evening. Suddenly he had discovered thousands of new friends and a promising new career, and during his remaining forty years that dry, drawling speech, with its tantalizing pause and droll payoff line, proved as profitable as his writing. Later it accomplished what his books could not do—it saved his honor and reputation.

At thirty-three he was thus well launched on his parallel careers of journalism and lecturing. He was also, it seemed, a confirmed bachelor. "I've never had the wish or time to bother with women," he told a friend. But one glance at a girl's picture changed all that. He was touring the Holy Land as a correspondent and aboard the *Quaker City* visited the stateroom of young Charles Langdon, where he saw an ivory miniature of a young girl, slender and frail, with large, dark eyes. "My sister Olivia," said Charles.

"She has the most beautiful face I've ever seen," said the awestruck Sam. "I could worship a girl like that." And he did, on sight. Forty years later he said, "From the first day I saw her, she has never been out of my mind."

Livy Langdon was a semi-invalid with a gentle voice and hair demurely parted in the middle. As flexible and giving as a spring, she had a happy, childlike laugh, but her character, like the spring, was made of steel and indestructibly fine. After Sam's first call on her, when he stayed thirteen hours, her deeply religious parents watched their adored daughter warily, for they had doubts about the rough-styled suitor with his pilot's profanity, his irreverence, and his taste for liquor and cigars. Though not exactly uncordial, they permitted him only enough correspondence so that Livy's piety might have an elevating effect upon him.

Thus began a series of love letters unique in American literature, so sacred, so private, that few people knew of their existence. Livy kept them locked in a green box for thirty-seven years and only after both were dead did the public see them. Burning with passion and entreaty during those frustrating days of waiting, still he could not be heavy-handed: "I do not regret that I love you; for once, I have seen the world all beautiful. But give me a little room in that great heart of yours. Write me something—texts from the New Testament, dissertations on smoking, *anything* . . ." he implored.

Her parents finally permitted him a week's visit in their handsome home in Elmira, New York—a week of well-chaperoned carriage drives and hymn-singing at the family piano —and when he had no excuse for staying longer, the Tom Sawyer in him came to his rescue. On the way to the station the carriage horse bolted, throwing him out on his head, and though he landed unharmed on a cushion of sand, he thought, Why waste such a gift from the gods? There he lay as one dead, a pitiable sight, and for days nothing soothed his agony save Livy's fingers stroking his brow.

When common politeness forced him to "recover," the daughter had softened considerably, but he still had the father to contend with. His charm was now no weapon, only raw character sufficing, and for her sake he made the supreme sacrifice by refraining from profanity and cigars. Further, at Mr. Langdon's request, Mark supplied the names of eighteen character witnesses, and was so thoroughly honest about it all that he almost wrecked his chances. Instead of his old cronies in the West who could be depended upon to give him a boost, he named respectable citizens—clergymen and schoolmasters—liable to tell the truth. After several months the square-jawed businessman with the mutton-chop whiskers sent for Mark. A sheaf of replies from the character witnesses lay before him and he read several aloud. All were gloomily negative. "Haven't you a friend in the world?" he demanded.

With his heart in his boots Mark replied, "Apparently not."

There was a long silence while Jervis Langdon studied him thoughtfully; then he smiled. "Well, I'll be your friend," he said. "I know you better than they do. Take the girl."

After this there was the matter of making enough money to support a wife, and to this end he lectured, corrected proof on a book he had written about the Holy Land, and, with a loan from Mr. Langdon, bought into a Buffalo newspaper. Finally in December his *The Innocents Abroad* came out and was immediately one of the most successful travel books ever published, bringing him over $1,200 a month. The wedding was set for February, 1870.

After the ceremony in Elmira a party of fifteen escorted the couple to Buffalo, where Mark had commissioned a friend to rent him rooms in a respectable boardinghouse. On arriving, however, they were driven to a mansion complete with cook, housemaid and coachman. The new husband growled with rage but Mr. Langdon, amid chucklings and gigglings from the wedding party, handed him a small box containing his wedding present—a deed to the house. So began this supremely happy marriage.

But finances were still a problem, for Mark would touch none of Livy's fortune and while money was pouring in on him, he sent it right out again, giving or spending with equal impetuosity. On one occasion during a lecture tour he became enraged at having to catch a two A.M. train and hired a locomotive to pick him up at a more reasonable hour. "Where does all this money I'm earning *go* to?" he stormed to Livy, but she was too tactful to tell him.

After the birth of their little boy they moved to Hartford, Connecticut. There Mark committed one of those unfortunate mistakes for which he was always being punished. Out riding with the baby one cold day, Mark let the covers slip from the infant's legs and he caught cold. Shortly afterward, diphtheria developed, and he died. Mark never forgave himself or, in an unreasoning way, the Policeman overhead Who had wielded such a vicious stick.

His writing career, however, continued to prosper, and it was at this time that he performed the trick of turning his father's Tennessee mountains into gold. Over dinner one evening at the home of Charles Dudley Warner, editor and essayist, the two men were reviling the current crop of novels so mercilessly that their wives dared them to do better. Thus challenged, they put the whole absurd, calamitous story of the mountain land into a novel, *The Gilded Age,* and it earned $20,000. Next they put its hero, a certain cousin of Mark's renamed Colonel Sellers, into a play and made $80,000 more. The only pity was that the poor judge, Mark's father, was not alive to see his initial investment pay off so handsomely.

Some of these earnings built the famous Mark Twain house in Hartford, where for seventeen years the wise, the witty, and the wealthy came and went. Here were born Clara and Jean, and here, between lecture tours, were written *Tom Sawyer, Huckleberry Finn, The Prince and the Pauper* and many others of Mark's best works. It was a happy time.

His method of composition was unique: there were always four or five stories going at once, and, getting started on one, he would race ahead with all the dash and fury of a fire truck until suddenly the fuel ran out. At first he was fearful that he had run dry; then he learned that if he put the piece aside for a while the tank would fill up again. *Tom Sawyer, The Prince and the Pauper* and *A Connecticut Yankee at the Court of King Arthur* all had two-year dry spells; *Huckleberry Finn* was on and off for eight; and *Captain Stormfield's Visit to Heaven* was forty years in the writing.

Ever since Mark's marriage he had submitted his books to Livy's editorial pencil and the rumor spread that she was a puritan dragon, deleting all the juiciest bits. But he too was partly responsible, amusing himself by pretending to be a henpecked husband, and most of the deletions were made in deference to a prevailing code that could see *Huck Finn* banned for the use of the phrase "go to hell."

In spite of Twain's robust humor, in spite of his tirades against orthodox churches, he was in reality a deeply religious man who was simply rebelling against the vengeful deity he had learned in boyhood. He rebelled, similarly, against all evil—injustice, tyranny, bigotry—using against them his own weapon of humor. "Irreverence," he said, "is the champion of liberty, its only sure defense. Humor must not *professedly* teach or preach, but actually it must do both if it would live forever."

Huckleberry Finn, with its character of the runaway slave Jim, was a plea for the underdog, a protest against the callousness of the privileged. Though slavery was officially dead, the spirit of slaveholding still persisted and Mark, remembering his old Negro friend Uncle Dan'l, was pleading through Jim for all the Uncle Dan'ls of the world.

A Connecticut Yankee, the idea of which came to him in a dream, was a lance leveled in defense of the poor and helpless, and though the setting was the Middle Ages, the point was for every age. W. D. Howells wrote of it: "There are incidents in this wonder-book which wring the heart, for the fantastic fable of Arthur's far-off time is too often the sad truth of our own."

Joan of Arc was a cry against injustice; *The Innocents Abroad* was a gibe at superstition; and so it went through all his books, the sharp bite softened by kindly laughter.

His fulminations against privileged wealth did not apply, of course, to wealth honestly earned, for having to support not only his own family but Orion's and his mother, he pursued money without shame. His ventures, unfortunately, were not buttressed by good judgment, and after refusing to invest in Alexander Graham Bell's voice-transmitting device, he kept on sinking fortunes in a worthless typesetting machine for fourteen years. In 1881 alone, he put $46,000 into various investments, of which $41,000 was pure loss.

About the same time, he went into publishing, having noticed the disparity between an author's profits and a publisher's, and he did very well with his first publication, which happened to be his own *Huckleberry Finn*. The memoirs of the current hero, General Ulysses Grant, likewise made him money, in spite of his insistence on paying Grant the highest royalty ever heard of. But that was the end of his publishing success; all else was disaster. For several years the losses piled up and at last, discouraged, bewildered, and ill from overwork and rheumatism, he turned the business over to others and moved to Europe and its cheaper living costs.

By then his daughters were nineteen, seventeen, and eleven—Susy the talented and charming, Clara the vivacious, Jean the beautiful. But Livy, still the loveliest and dearest, was not well. Something was wrong with her heart, and it was thought travel might help. For many months they wandered, finally settling in a twenty-eight-room villa near Florence, where he wrote frantically to catch up on his debts. But books could not save him now, for the 1893 financial panic in the United States was wiping out income from everything of the sort. Livy put up the last of her own money to save the publishing firm, but it was too late. Mark, $100,000 in debt, had to declare himself bankrupt. The shame nearly killed them both.

In terror they turned to their millionaire friend Henry Rogers, an American financier. Livy had wanted to turn over everything to the ninety-six creditors and apologize to boot, but while Rogers agreed to the apologies he insisted on retaining the copyrights in Mark's fifteen books. Mark still believed his beloved typesetting invention might save the day, but when a final test washed that out, the entire $190,000 he had put into it went with the rest. According to law, bankrupts were not obligated to repay creditors, but not being moral bankrupts Mark and Livy resolved that each of the ninety-six printers, ink dealers, papermakers and bookbinders must be repaid. The one quick, sure way to do so was by lecturing, and at sixty Mark started on a thirteen-month world tour. Jean was too young to go along, Susy was not very well and wanted to continue her singing lessons at home. So Livy and Clara went with Mark. He sent the proceeds back to Rogers regularly and, after the trip, wrote its story in *Following the Equator,* with the result that after three and a half years Rogers finally cabled CREDITORS HAVE ALL BEEN PAID ONE HUNDRED CENTS ON THE DOLLAR. Mark could now face America again.

The story of his failure being well known, this triumph was greeted with many editorials saluting his integrity and courage, and as he stepped off the steamer he said to the welcoming reporters, "I'm so glad to be back I'm going to break both my legs so I can't ever get away again."

Thus his money troubles were behind him; but now other cares, a perfect storm of them, began beating down. His greatest blessing had been his family, but one by one he saw them go, and the courage that had supported him seemed to disintegrate. Susy, the oldest daughter, was the first. Shortly after the tour had ended, word came to them in London that she was ill, and four days later a cable followed: SUSY WAS RELEASED FROM MENINGITIS PEACEFULLY LAST NIGHT.

As usual Mark took the blame on himself: if he had made her come with him, if he had done this or not done that, Susy would be alive. "It is one of the mysteries of nature," he cried, "that a man, all unprepared, can receive a thunder-stroke like that and live." But steadied by Livy's courage and devotion, he survived, though for long there was no laughter in the house, and no birthday, no Christmas holiday or any other day of celebration was recognized—Susy had made so much of holidays.

In an effort to find help for Livy, the family moved about

restlessly—London, Switzerland, Vienna, Budapest, Sweden—but none of these places did her much good and in 1903 they went back to the sun of Florence. There Jean and Clara nursed their ill mother for a year while Mark, limited to two minutes a day with her because his presence was too exciting, hung about her door like a lost soul. He wrote furiously because he had to, but his heart was inside the room.

On June 5, 1904, Livy died quietly, loved by her husband as only the most fortunate of women are loved. She had taken Susy's death without complaint, but Mark had no such restraint and he thrashed out against this cruel persecution.

But the more he railed, the fiercer seemed to blow the storms: Clara collapsed after her mother's death and spent many months in a rest home; Jean, long subject to epilepsy, was forced to do likewise. Then his best friend, Rogers, died. He could not understand such cruelty.

Fortunately he was surrounded by good and loving friends who softened his private griefs in many ways. There was comfort, too, in the honorary degree accorded him by Oxford University, in Clara's marriage to the great musician Ossip Gabrilowitsch, and in the friendship of many little girls, with whom he relived his own daughters' childhood. So far, indeed, did one child melt his bitterness that when, not knowing his dread of holidays, she brought him a gift and cried, "Merry Christmas," he was able to return, "And a merry Christmas to you." It was the first time since Susy's death thirteen years before that he had acknowledged its existence.

But he could never quite forgive Christmas, for it brought him the final blow. After two years in a hospital, Jean came home in late December to share a real celebration with festive tree and presents. But the excitement was too much and after a lively evening of preparation, she was found the next morning in her room, dead. This time he was not violent with grief, only numb, perhaps because he had worried about leaving this sick girl alone and now at least that fear was past.

Mark Twain

Mark, the aging, cynical man, was tired of life and very lonely with Livy and his girls gone, for Clara was in Europe with her husband. But the other Mark, the Tom Sawyer one, still lifted his perky head. After Jean's death he wrote: "Shall I ever be cheerful again?" and he answered himself, "Yes." He knew himself, knew that laughter was his other self and that until he died he would relish the humor of life.

But, like Livy, there was something the matter with his heart and finally it gave out. He had looked forward to this event not without longing, for he had often said, "Oh, how I wish I was with Livy," and after six years of separation the wish came true.

Robert Louis Stevenson

(1850=1894)

Robert Louis Stevenson

(1850=1894)

RLS. For many years these were the best-known, best-loved initials in the world of letters. Since then both the writer R. L. Stevenson, and the man Louis, have undergone a change in the public's esteem—the writer being first glorified and then "debunked" and the man idolized and then "exposed." For all estimates of him to be true he would have to be his own Dr. Jekyll and Mr. Hyde, and though today opinions are less extreme, the controversies remain, as well as a certain mystery.

What sort of writer *was* RLS? What might he have become? And his wife—was the fierce and courageous little Tiger Lily ballast or balloon? The last paragraph he ever wrote may hold the answers.

But first came the years when the questions took shape, the years that began on November 13, 1850. RLS's mother, Margaret Balfour, came of eminent folk—ministers, doctors and the like. His father, Thomas Stevenson, was third in the line of famous engineers who built the lighthouses guarding the coasts of Scotland. Both had twelve brothers and sisters, but after that the large families ceased, for delicate Meg Stevenson was given to colds and fevers and one baby was all she could manage.

Little Lou, as RLS was called, was accustomed to sickness as a way of life. He was barely three when he asked his mother gravely, "Do you think I'm looking very ill?" and forty-one years later the same question was his final utterance. All the years between, this question of his health was a refrain dictated by one of the most unstable physiques a man ever had to put up with.

He was a thin child with large dark eyes set abnormally far apart, and in the raw cold of Edinburgh, a city farther north than the Aleutians, he was forever chilled to the bone, forever sniffling and sneezing and being put to bed. The rattling of the windowpanes sent the nervous child into sweating tremors at night, and many an hour the father sat outside the boy's door murmuring softly till the comforting drone had soothed him to sleep.

Kind and good was the father, loving the mother, but it was nurse Alison Cunningham, a handsome fisherman's daughter, who was companion, teacher, playmate and shield against the world. Fond of a joke and a good Scots story, "Cummy" dosed him, bundled him in blankets, and read to him by the hour. And Lou, steeped in her ferocious Calvinist theology, played at ministers as others play at Indians, worrying about the souls of sheep and horses and begging that the Bible be read to them at once.

This Calvinism was strong meat for a nervous child. "I can remember," he said later, "repeatedly waking from a dream of Hell, clinging to the bar of my bed, my body convulsed with agony." But he learned early to live with fear, even relishing the drama of pure terror, and with a toy theatre on the bed acted out thrilling robberies and murders, raids by pirates and highwaymen. In summer, when his solitude was relieved by visits with many cousins in numerous country houses, the adventures became real-life ones, adventures which he faced with teeth chattering but heart reckless and unquailing. The courage he developed in himself served him well in later life.

The writing began at four or five with "songstries" which

ROBERT L. STEVENSON
(ca. 1882)

he gabbled to himself (and which his father wrote down from behind the door), and at six he gravely dictated a History of Moses to his mother. Soon came a conscious decision to be a writer. For that, one did exercises as a musician does scales, studying a man or a cloud or a caterpillar till he could transfer its precise appearance and movement onto paper. Everything he saw or did went into a notebook and every author contributed to his style. "When I read a book or passage with some distinction," he said later, "I must sit down at once and ape that quality. Thus I got practice in harmony, in rhythm, and in construction, playing the sedulous ape to Lamb, to Wordsworth, to Defoe, to Hawthorne, to Baudelaire."

What with illness and travel abroad, he had little formal education, and that he disliked. Impatient of the hearty athletics of school life, he preferred to wander off alone dreaming and scribbling, while his long stringy body, narrow of shoulder and flat of chest, made him an object of derision to the other boys. They kept apart in mutual disgust. But come college time, he was naturally expected to carry on the Stevenson tradition, and so dutifully he enrolled at Edinburgh University in 1867.

There were difficulties then, for, asserting his independence, he went about with lank shoulder-length hair, shabby black velvet jacket, duck trousers halfway up his bony calves, and tie resembling a scrap of dirty carpet. Alert and questing as a spaniel, his mind was always darting after some fancy, and he annoyed his colleagues with his eternal "suppose this was to happen," and "suppose that happened next." It was not until his popular cousin Bob Stevenson ran interference for him that his classmates saw the charm behind the eccentricity.

Bob Stevenson, an art student with three years in Paris back of him, was a rare and soaring spirit, "the very best talker in the whole world," Lou said. He opened the way for his cousin and then the younger, riding his own dazzling wit, swept past and took the lead.

This new popularity brought Lou the courage to adopt fresh ideas and the boldness to stand by them, both of which he needed, for his father had assumed without wondering that the Stevenson tradition was in safe hands. Lou had made a sincere stab at cooperating in the engineering profession, but daily he cared less for the dynamics of mineral debris under stress of moving water and more for the dynamics of words. Finally he knew that his course was directed by a force more compelling than duty.

The time came when Mr. Stevenson must be told, and one day, on a "dreadful walk," the incredulous man learned that his life's plan had faded into mist. There were arguments and storms in which the mansion at 17 Heriot Row was alternately chilly and ablaze, but a compromise was finally effected: Lou might try his hand with words if at the same time he would adopt a solid profession—read for the law, say—as a standby, just in case.

This was not the parents' only cause for concern, for while their friends' sons were marrying respectably in St. Giles Cathedral, theirs was spending his time no one knew where. When he did attend a formal function he appeared in those appalling clothes that only advertised his defection. This decent couple could only suspect the sinister influence of that quarter known as the Old Town.

These suspicions were well-founded. A burning interest in people, an equalizing respect for all, and a certain curiosity about the forbidden drew Louis to this reeking slum to fraternize with thieves, prostitutes, and drunkards. An ardent, lusty youth despite his frail appearance, he could not feel that sensuality necessarily was a sin; he regarded malice, unkindness, and cowardice as greater vices.

Nevertheless, he was a product of his times, when sex was considered indecent and unmentionable, and in spite of himself he shared the common confusion and distress.

This Victorian period was almost unique, in that for most of a century a whole population wrestled with itself in an effort to live a life of purity and rectitude beyond human powers of achievement. The effort was backbreaking, the failure heartbreaking—and inevitable. But the intensity of the desire made the failure proportionately painful, and "Victorian hypocrisy" was the result, a covering up of the sinfulness they could neither conquer nor bear to admit.

The mood of the period caused a second grueling conflict in the Stevenson family. Christian theology held with the first chapter of Genesis that the universe had been created complete in six days. But in 1859, Charles Darwin had published his *Origin of Species* with its revolutionary theory of evolution, and this neat universe was shattered like glass. The shock was staggering, and Christians whose lives had been rooted in an unquestioning faith either rejected it out of hand or, unwillingly convinced, found themselves torn from their roots and floating in a void. Both sides suffered intensely—and the Stevenson family found themselves on opposite sides.

RLS, young, intellectual, ardent, had joined Edinburgh University's Speculative Society, where the members wrestled with the day's burning issues, and, having suffered terrors as a child from Cummy's fundamentalism, he now swung from doubting nothing to doubting all. He spared his parents this uncomfortable knowledge at first, but when his father found an incriminating paper and put to him one or two sharp questions, he confessed all and the fat was in the fire.

The sequel was so lacerating that he admitted to a friend: "If I had foreseen the hell since, I think I should have lied. I had thought of my father but I had forgotten my mother, and now they are both ill, both silent. If it were not too late I would almost retract. But am I to live my whole life as a falsehood? I am, I think, as honest as they, I have not come hastily to my views, and I don't think I should be called a horrible atheist. But what a damned curse I am to them! My father said, 'You have rendered my whole life a failure,' and my mother, 'This is the heaviest affliction that has ever befallen me.'"

For months poor Mr. Stevenson could not let it alone, studying theologians' tracts on the recovery of lost souls, praying loudly and pointedly at his son, even shutting the door on his nephew Bob as a sinister influence in the home. And Mrs. Stevenson more than once collapsed in hysterics. The worst of it was that they were all so dear to each other; in the midst of the wrangling Lou groaned, "I can't help getting friendly with my father, I do love him so."

A welcome respite from the strain came through the introduction of a new element in Louis' life. Frances Sitwell was a strikingly beautiful woman, eleven years his senior and the wife of an Episcopalian minister. Separated, though not divorced, she was working as secretary of a London college. Having recently suffered the loss of her younger son, she had brought the older one with her for a recuperative visit to her friend, Mrs. Churchill Babington, at Cambridge University. One day Mrs. Babington said to her guest, "I am expecting a young Balfour cousin of mine, a nice young fellow, very clever, and I think you will like him." That afternoon at teatime RLS, a lean twenty-two in a velvet jacket, entered the room, looked at the divinity on the sofa, and fell in love.

Fanny Sitwell, with her oriental eyes and Mona Lisa mouth, was always surrounded by a circle of men distractedly in love, particularly young and literary ones. Still, she managed to maintain a virtue unassailable and unquestioned, somehow holding the frantic men in check until, like horses gently broken, they accepted her terms and remained her friends for life.

Thus it was with Louis. Ablaze with excitement he burst into fireworks of talk, and after listening for a few amazed hours she sent word to her friend Sidney Colvin: "Come at once if you want to meet an unmistakable young genius. His conversation is like nothing I ever heard before."

Colvin was a twenty-eight-year-old Cambridge professor, essayist and art critic who was to become curator of prints at the British Museum—and thirty years later, when Fanny was free—to win her in marriage. Obeying her summons, he came; and he too fell under Louis' spell. "This youngster," he cried in wonder, "seemed already to have lived and seen and felt and laughed more than others do in a lifetime. Riotous freaks of fancy, grave argument, flashes of nonsense, streamed from him in a strong Scottish accent." He made the thin, slovenly skeleton his protégé, reading Louis' articles and using his influence to get them in the proper magazines. No jealousy marring the friendship, he served as Louis' adviser and critic in life, and his literary executor after death.

Mrs. Sitwell proved the perfect confidante, and when Louis returned to Edinburgh he wrote her, "I want our friendship, my own dearest friend, to be the faithfulest, most candid that has ever been." Of the family's theological struggles he wrote her: "This is a trial of nervous strength between my father and me, and the weaker will die first. Either alternative is horrible." Then one day he reported in relief, "The Lord Advocate, a friend of my father's, strongly advised me in his hearing to go to the English bar. The chief law officer's advice goes a long way here." And so to London and the law it was, in utter thanksgiving.

But the months of wrangling had worn his five foot ten inches down to 118 pounds, and on his arrival Mrs. Sitwell sent for a specialist, who named the trouble nervous exhaustion but privately feared tuberculosis as well. At any rate, he said there was to be no nonsense about wintering in this vile climate, and off to the Riviera Stevenson went, his frightened parents subsidizing him.

RLS was a writer who never let an experience go to waste, and this flight from death provided him with the theme for the essay "Ordered South," while "Lay Morals" expressed his qualms about accepting a loan he might not live to repay. So sensitive was his conscience on this point that he almost starved himself until Colvin arrived for an inspection and laid down the law on the use of good sense.

In his weak and vulnerable condition, Louis fell into another curious relationship with not one older woman but two. Russian noblewomen and sisters, they flirted and teased in French, darting and swooping like birds of paradise and calling him a sweet young Scottish genius. Of one of them, who professed more than motherly interest in him, he wrote to Mrs. Sitwell in flattered bewilderment; nevertheless, he remained faithful to his "dearest friend" and the Riviera flirtation came to nothing.

In the spring he returned to Edinburgh, where his parents were so grateful to see their skeleton son filled out and brown that they dropped the Genesis versus Darwin argument and promised him not only a small allowance but a thousand pounds when he passed his law examinations. After this turn, hastening to London, he laid himself at his lady's feet.

In his renewed vigor he let himself get dangerously out of hand, but her tact was equal to the emergency. A married woman, she reminded him, and one eleven years too old, was not for the likes of him, but her unbounded affection and admiration she could and would gladly give. Perforce he accepted her conditions and by degrees one kind of love was transmuted into another, until he was addressing her as "Madonna" and "Mother" and apologizing for the selfish baby he had been. On this safe ground they remained friends until his death.

These two feminine encounters, the English and the Russian, formed parts of a larger pattern. Older women attracted him always; and a third, this time an American, was to become the pivotal woman in his life. Meanwhile he had to meet the pivotal man. These two would tear him apart between them.

Louis' daily prayer was for health, money and friendships, the first two of which came in reasonable amounts, while the third was a veritable flood.

He had sold a number of pieces to the *Cornhill* Magazine, and its editor, passing through town, took him to see a young poet lying ill in Edinburgh Infirmary. W. E. Henley, red of hair and boisterous of wit, with not a penny to his name, had lost one foot to tuberculosis of the bone and was there now to beg the great Joseph Lister, pioneer of asepsis, to save the other. The treatment was long and agonizing, but Henley met it with a courage expressed in his famous poem "Invictus"—*I am the master of my fate, I am the captain of my soul.*

He and RLS took to each other on sight, and the talk was riotous for days. As soon as Henley could sit up, Louis, temporarily out of cab fare, carried an armchair to him on his head, and a few weeks later he wrote Mrs. Sitwell:

> I took him on his first carriage drive yesterday. I had a business to carry him down the long stairs and more to get him up again, but it is now the top of the spring here and the whole country is mad with green. You can imagine what it was to a man eighteen months in a ward. The look of his face was as wine to me.

Their affection exalted them both. Years afterward, Louis drew a portrait of Henley as John Silver in *Treasure Island* and Henley drew Louis in *Apparition,* thus: "Thin legged, thin chested, the brown eyes radiant with vivacity—there shines a brilliant and romantic grace, with trace on trace of passion, impudence and energy." When Louis was ill, Henley nursed him in his own grimy lodgings, and when Henley needed money Louis lent it freely. Louis introduced Henley to Colvin's influential set and Henley, later influential himself, acted as Louis' unpaid agent for years.

By now twenty-five and selling his writings fairly regularly, Louis made a decisive announcement to his parents: no law practice, no settling down. "I am a hopeless tramp," he told them. And so he proved to be, going on walking and boating trips through France with Sir Walter Simpson and, with his cousin Bob Stevenson, exploring, by count, two hundred and ten European towns. At the Barbizon artists' colony outside Paris he became one of its famed Bohemian set, dressing and talking in so bizarre a manner that a well-attired friend, meeting him on the street, refused to stop. "My character will stand a great deal," he said, "but it won't stand being seen talking to a thing like you."

For Louis it was a matchless time of work, freedom, and hilarious companionships. He cherished his bachelorhood and when his friends fell away he wrote distrustingly of marriage: "It is a step so grave that it attracts light-headed men by its very awfulness." Yet at this moment he himself was sliding toward the same fate.

Having written for accommodations with Simpson and Bob at a country inn near Paris, he was outraged to find already ensconced there an American woman with a daughter and son. "This is the beginning of the end," he wailed. And in truth it was.

Fanny Vandegrift Osbourne, born in Indianapolis, Indiana, in 1840, had left her husband, a good-natured, feckless Kentuckian, after repeated infidelities, and had brought her seventeen-year-old Belle and eight-year-old Lloyd to France. There had been another son, but he had died recently, and it was to recover from the shock of his death that Fanny had come to Grez.

To Louis all this was a curious echo of that other Fanny— the Fanny Sitwell of his impressionable youth. There was the same name, the same wide difference in their ages, the same unhappy marriage, even the same recent loss of a son. The similarity stopped there, however, for the two women were vastly different in disposition. Fanny Osbourne was a short, stocky, dark woman with a face like a young Napoleon in its classic beauty and masculine expression. She could cook, sew, ride, roll a cigarette, shoot, and get her own way with Napoleonic force; also she was gifted in writing, painting, playing the piano, and, on occasion, seeing into the future. A diminutive powder magazine.

Painting was Fanny's excuse for coming to France, and economy the reason for her choosing Grez. Belle's girlish beauty immediately captivated a host of males, but Louis was drawn more to Fanny's stories of the West and its gold-miners and Indians. The friendship grew apace; by the following summer the hypnotized young man was carrying Fanny's painting outfit, paddling her canoe, and making his brilliant humorous talk. Against her will she too was charmed and attracted, and without any sudden moment of revelation the two realized they were in love.

The following winter in Paris, Louis developed an eye infection and Fanny, disregarding all talk, installed him in her apartment to take over the nursing. Thus began their sixteen harrowing years together and since, with her usual clairvoyance, she knew already of the greater illness that was to come, she was thereby exhibiting a certain conscious courage. But courage was one thing Fanny never lacked.

While taking him to London for eye treatment, she was introduced to Sidney Colvin, Fanny Sitwell, and Henley, who were promptly appointed by Louis as ambassadors to his parents in Edinburgh. But the news they had to convey was ambiguous at best, since no engagement could be announced until Fanny Osbourne was free. She tried divorce negotiations by cable and mail, but Sam Osbourne proved stubborn and at last she was compelled to sail for America with her children. Louis fidgeted in London for a year, while his parents in Scotland gritted their teeth and prayed.

In curious contrast to his usual torrential letter writing, Louis could write to Fanny hardly at all. "All that people want by letters has been done between us," he said, "but still

I can do no work." Then in the thirteenth month came a cablegram from her. No one except Louis ever saw it, but he told his friends that Fanny was ill and he must go to her at once.

His parents were stunned by this turn after such a promising silence, and Mr. Stevenson cried out, "Is it fair that we should be half murdered by this sinful mad business? I lay it all at the door of Darwin, unsettling a man's faith in such serious matters." For a while they considered leaving Scotland to escape the gossip.

Meanwhile Louis' friends pressed their own arguments against his contemplated trip: he was poor; he was ill; his disappearance from the literary scene at this time would ruin his career; and the woman might never really get the divorce. Nodding, he listened, and invited them to see him off at St. Pancras Station.

Traveling without help from his parents, he sailed third class and spent the ten nights it took to cross the United States sleeping on a bare board in suffocating heat and odors. On reaching California lugging a ten-volume history of the United States, he collapsed and nearly died.

Somehow he got to Monterey and found Fanny still ill but recovering. For eight miserable months, while they waited for the divorce, he lodged in dingy rooms near her house and ate at a small, friendly restaurant for forty-five cents a day. There, unknown to himself, his winning charm saved his life, for his fellow boarders secretly paid a local paper two dollars a week to give him work.

During this period the long-suspected tuberculosis became a certainty, and at a time when the disease generally meant death, Louis and Fanny met his sentence in typical fashion, she grimly defiant, he gallant and unbroken.

The illness brought extra expenses, and in deep need Louis wrote to an Edinburgh friend, Charles Baxter, asking that he sell his books for him. When his father learned of his plight, pity blotted out anger and he cabled his son: COUNT ON £ 250 A YEAR. Such a windfall Louis was not quite heroic enough to refuse, saying, "I am not very likely to make my fortune as an author, and I may never even see next spring."

At last the divorce was accomplished and the two were married. Mr. Stevenson's gift enabled them to rent a honeymoon cabin at an abandoned California silver mine—later described by Louis in *The Silverado Squatters*.

Returning to England after a year's absence, Louis found his parents and friends resigned to making the best of the marriage. Fanny too was conciliatory, joking carefully with her father-in-law and accepting with grace her mother-in-law's gifts. They in turn were surprised and gratified, for though she was a divorcee and ten years older than their son, at least she put on no airs and only laughed when people mistook her for his mother. And it was obvious to them that she would look out for his health.

Louis and his friends were delirious over their reunion, drinking and smoking and talking all night—Bob Stevenson, brilliant and garrulous, Henley boisterously possessive, Edmund Gosse nodding critically, Colvin chuckling and clucking. Fanny was all cordiality at first, but as these late sessions ran on she sank into a baleful silence, her brooding eyes sliding resentfully from one to another. Would they never go home? They were using up his strength. Nothing was said, but the tug-of-war had begun, a mute battle between the possessors, his friends, and the intruder, his wife.

When the question arose of where the couple should settle, Louis vetoed London and its climate. Fanny, who was determined to get him away, favored Davos, the new Swiss TB resort. So began a seven-year search for a home, Davos for two winters, then the Riviera, and finally two years in a chalet in the south of France. Nothing seemed quite right.

Finally the love between father and son that no disputes

could kill called them back to England. The older man's health was failing, so Fanny and Louis settled on the fashionable south coast of England where—so far had Fanny's charms succeeded—Mr. Stevenson actually made her a present of a house.

During those previous seven restless resort years Louis' writing style had become more clear and simple and his literary career now took definite form. Fanny passed on each day's work, either as it was read aloud or was sent to her room for comments, and though they often argued hotly, she almost always won.

The extent of Fanny's editorial influence is a question to the present day. Louis had made a few tries at a powerful love story but, with the Victorian reader in mind, she had not approved of his less than pure women characters. Finally he gave up the attempt; if he could not write the story honestly he would not do it at all. His books as a consequence are short on women and mature relationships between the sexes.

This has been called the tragedy of RLS, the tragedy of a man cheated of greatness by pressures fencing him in. It may be that he was indeed thus cheated. But there are indications that if he had lived longer he might have jumped that fence.

Any work was a strain on this skeleton frame, and though Louis did much of his writing in bed, littering the covers with papers and the makings of hand-rolled cigarettes, he was forbidden at times to speak or move for his lungs' sake. Then he lay with his arms strapped to his side to avert a hemorrhage, while Fanny jumped for medicine at the first sign of one. "This not being able to read or speak," he complained wryly, "this being too weak to write and too bored to eat, leaves a man some empty hours. A fortnight of silence, of not stirring my right hand, is devilish like being dead. Still, I can live with joy in the art by which I support myself.

Robert Louis Stevenson

I have the best wife in the world, and my friends are many and true-hearted. It is a big thing in successes, really."

This gallantry, this irrepressible spirit, brought him his first wide popularity. His stepson Lloyd Osbourne had been taken out of boarding school for lack of funds, and Louis, always ready for an hour's play, began drawing him a map of an imaginary island dotted with colorful names—Skeleton Island, Spyglass Hill, and so on. The island needed a story to go with it and he began spinning one, eventually catching a feeling of excitement himself and putting it all down on paper. A friend suggested he try sending it to a boy's magazine, and though the first installments created no great stir, interest grew as it progressed, and with book publication the story, *Treasure Island,* came into real money. "A hundred jingling, tingling, golden minted pounds, a lot more than the yarn is worth but very pleasant notwithstanding," he cried in jubilation.

Enchanted with this new juvenile audience, RLS followed with *The Black Arrow,* and *A Child's Garden of Verses,* dedicating these nostalgic poems to the "Cummy" who had been the center of his childhood. Then in 1886 came the piece that made him world-famous.

Louis' plots often came to him in dreams, gifts of that subconscious mind which he called his "brownies" and on which many writers depend to take their raw notions and shape them overnight. He had been steeping himself in Poe's stories of the supernatural, at the same time pondering the duality of man's nature. One night the two coalesced and, accidentally awakened by Fanny, he cried out, "Oh, you've broken off a fine bogey-tale." In the morning he sat down to his desk in feverish excitement and three days later, *Dr. Jekyll and Mr. Hyde* was on paper.

The story, laying bare the strife between good and evil inside every man, instantly struck a responsive note in multitudes of readers. As a sure sign of its universality, the two names became symbols, labels, and eventually part of the English language.

This brilliant turn came at a good time, for Louis had been in a black mood over his own health, his father's mental deterioration, and the bad reviews of a recent book, *Prince Otto*. Success was good medicine for the blues, and he briskly dashed off a sequel to *Treasure Island*. With the publication of *Kidnapped* money really began rolling in.

The following year his father's death, after a long illness, broke the bonds with England, and Louis and Fanny set their minds on travel. Fanny's wish was to see America again, Louis' to find a beneficial climate, Mrs. Stevenson's to escape the old, familiar scenes, and Lloyd's to go wherever Louis went. In August, 1887, the family headed vaguely toward the west.

Surprises met them in New York where Louis, it turned out, was famous. Richard Mansfield's stage version of *Jekyll and Hyde* was just opening, and they were met at the boat by a host of reporters. E. L. Burlingame of *Scribner's* magazine offered $3,500 for twelve essays, and S. S. McClure of *McClure's* magazine topped that with $10,000 for fifty-two columns. The larger offer was, Louis declared, more than he was worth, but he closed with Scribner's and made a number of satisfactory deals for his books. Socially, they were enveloped by friends who declared that the Far West was poor TB country compared with the nearby Adirondacks, so they rented a "hatbox on a hill" in Saranac and wintered in weather forty degrees below zero.

During these frigid months RLS wrote little beyond the contracted essays and a story on which he collaborated with Lloyd Osbourne. His chief activity was the consideration of Samuel McClure's various proposals, one of which was to change all their lives. Sea voyages had always seemed good medicine for Louis, and while the blizzards raged outside their "hatbox," the family often sat dreaming aloud of a yachting trip in the tropics. Once McClure, listening to this talk, leaped with excitement. "How much for a weekly travel letter from far-off places?" he asked. Louis suggested a hundred dollars, McClure doubled the figure and, money now being only the pleasantest of his problems, Louis and Lloyd began buying up maps. Fanny, at fifty, and Mrs. Stevenson, at sixty, were equally game for such a trip, and the French maid, Valentine, agreed to go along. In the spring Fanny went to San Francisco yacht-hunting. While she was gone, Louis suffered his most painful experience.

The friendship with W. E. Henley had been a mainstay of Louis' life, though, as Fanny said, he was coarse, possessive, and given to guzzling their whiskey. But he had aided RLS generously as unpaid agent and sounding board. Above all, he had loved him with his whole rough heart. Unfortunately he also detested Fanny; and subconsciously he may have resented Louis' expanding success. Anyway, he now seized upon a small matter to make large trouble.

The previous year a mutual friend had shown Henley and the Stevensons a story she had written. Fanny, who had sold one or two yarns and fancied herself as a writer, suggested some changes. The writer rejected them and sent out the story as it was. When it failed to sell, she wrote Fanny, "Take the idea and rewrite it as you choose." This Fanny did, selling it to Scribner's under her own name as sole author.

Such was the small matter, the kernel of the trouble. Henley, in London, saw the magazine, recognized the plot, and wrote Louis accusing Fanny of plagiarism. RLS was famous for the occasional ferocity of his temper, and now the explosion shook the atmosphere like a bomb: Henley knew full well Fanny had been given the plot. Retract the charge, he demanded across the Atlantic. But Henley failed to retract. Accusations multiplied, friends took sides, everyone felt miserable, and the famous friendship became a famous quarrel.

The whole destructive affair drove Louis nearly to suicide, and he never felt quite wholehearted about anyone again. Still, there was in him a loyalty that could not break a friendship entirely, and he instructed Charles Baxter, who was handling his English affairs, to keep an eye on Henley and, at the first sign of want, to provide him with a small monthly allowance. It was to be done anonymously, of course.

This loyalty was not repaid in kind, and, fortunately for Louis, he was to be spared the most damaging part of the story. Seven years after his death a cousin wrote an adulatory biography of him. Henley, reviewing it, protested that its subject—this "barley-sugar effigy"—had been in fact vain, stingy, self-centered and affected. The attack infuriated Louis' friends and a controversy ensued—was he devil or angel?—that has never since entirely subsided.

During this stormy period Fanny wired from San Francisco: CAN SECURE SPLENDID SEAGOING SCHOONER YACHT CASCO FOR $750 A MONTH WITH MOST COMFORTABLE ACCOMMODATIONS FOR SIX AFT AND SIX FORWARD. REPLY IMMEDIATELY. Relieved to bury Henley at sea, Louis closed the cottage and rushed west with Lloyd, Mrs. Stevenson and Valentine.

The owner of the ninety-four-foot *Casco* retreated in alarm when he saw the bag of loose bones, the stately *grande dame*, the twenty-year-old boy and the French maid, but Louis' charm as usual won him over, and the captain as well. Nevertheless, the latter did dubiously study Louis' pallor and make private provision for a burial at sea.

In June, 1888, the party sailed for the South Pacific, the women wearing, on local advice, long loose muumuus in place of the usual corsets and tight-fitting dresses. After a month's cruise and two hurricanes, through which the women gritted their teeth and Louis grinned and exulted, they stopped at the Marquesas Islands and then moved on to Tahiti. There Captain Otis' expectations were nearly fulfilled when Louis, near death, called him to his bedside and, calmly smoking a cigarette, gave precise orders regarding the care of ship and passengers in the event of his demise. He surprised everyone by recovering, at the same time establishing a loving relationship with the local nobility that left the island in tears when the *Casco* departed.

In Honolulu, where they were met by Fanny's daughter, Belle, and her artist husband, Joe Strong, they took root long enough for Louis to write *The Master of Ballantrae*, after which they set out again, finally fetching up at Samoa. The party was a strange sight wandering down the main street of Apia, RLS in dirty shorts with a flute in hand, Lloyd with a ukulele, and Fanny, in her muumuu, with a guitar. At first they were taken for a broken-down theatrical troup, but the RLS name opened all doors and when a prominent citizen introduced them around, the decision to settle there soon followed.

Now Louis wrote to Henry James:

> I shall only come home once more, to die. Health I enjoy in the tropics. The sea, the climate, the island and the islanders, make me truly happy, and here there is a direct mail service to Europe, which is very important. I am sorry about seven or eight people in Europe and one or two in the States, but outside of that I simply prefer Samoa. I have bought 314 acres of beautiful land fifteen hundred feet above Apia, with streams, waterfalls, a great view of forest, sea and mountains, and fifty head of cattle. When we get a house built and a garden laid it might even bring in a little income.

The house they built, which they called "Vailima," was a large wooden structure, luxurious by South Sea standards, and in time it acquired the piano, the massive furniture and silver and glass of the Edinburgh house. It also boasted nineteen servants, naked to the waist for everyday work and, for festivities, draped in sarongs of Royal Stewart plaid.

This voluntary exile of a Scotsman in a strange and exotic land excited the imagination of the world and brought travelers from afar to have a look at him. Visitors were always welcome, and, urging J. M. Barrie to come, Louis described what the visitor would find:

> SELF: beginning to be grizzled, general appearance of a blasted boy. Past, eccentric; present, industrious, respectable and contented. Name in family, The Tame Celebrity. Hopelessly entangled in apron strings. Drinks plenty, curses some, temper unstable. Has been an invalid for ten years but you can't tell it on him. Given to explaining the universe. Scotch, sir, Scotch. BELLE: Runs me like a baby, sees I'm properly dressed, looks after me from taking my dictation to trimming my nails. FANNY: Runs the show. Infinitely little, gray curls, insane black eyes, tiny bare feet, native dress, cigarette. Hellish energy, doctors everybody. A violent friend and brimstone enemy. Is always either loathed or slavishly adored. Dreams dreams and sees visions. The Tiger Lily.

How could any traveler resist? The narrow rocky path up the hill, that path that was to become so famous, was worn by innumerable foreign feet.

And by native feet as well. Locally he was "Tusitala," Teller of Tales, and to the Samoans, whom he called God's sweetest work, he was less boss than chief of the clan. Once, accepting an outstanding omelet from the cook, he bowed ceremoniously and said, "Great is your wisdom."

"Great is my love," was the reply.

Much time was spent, as lawgiver and judge, adjudicating some quarrel or receiving some chieftain with *kava* and oratory flowing, and inevitably he became involved in local politics. Germany, an expanding power with its eye on Samoa, was setting the chieftains at each other's throats, and there were jailings, dynamitings, finally a small war, and

Louis indignantly threw his weight to the rightful ruler, Mataafa. Chairing meetings of white citizens, he drafted protests and wrote letters to the *Times* of London, while his family, dressed to the nines, brought impressive gifts to "beautiful, sweet old Mataafa" in jail. Such was Louis' prestige that the imprisoned chieftains were released, and in return he received one of the most touching—and celebrated —gifts ever tendered a friend.

The path up to Vailima was a narrow rocky trail, hard on the feet of horse and man alike, but now Mataafa's seventeen chieftains, men who had never stooped to manual work in their lives, set to with pickaxes and saws. Down came trees, up came rocks, away went tons of rubble. In a month a broad smooth road ran up the side of the mountain, and at its entrance stood a sign bearing seventeen names:

WE BEAR IN MIND THE SURPASSING KINDNESS OF MR. R. L. STEVENSON AND HIS LOVING CARE DURING OUR TRIBULATIONS WHILE IN PRISON. WE HAVE THEREFORE PREPARED A TYPE OF GIFT THAT WILL ENDURE WITHOUT DECAY FOREVER—THE ROAD WE HAVE CONSTRUCTED.

They called it The Road of the Loving Heart.

By now this love was shared by uncounted thousands around the world, winning him the name of "the best-loved writer of his generation." But underneath the applause ran a rumble of dissent—was he not too much the perennial boy? Action and adventure were all very good, but, to be really great, mustn't a writer produce at least one towering love story, portray one memorable woman? Stevenson had long been conscious of this lack, excusing himself with "the times are not ripe," and "I don't dare." But now in his forty-fifth year he jumped the fence that Fanny and the Victorians had thrown up around him. Whether they liked it or not, he would write the story that had been nagging him for years, a story of two Scotsmen and their women, tragic and weak, abrading themselves upon each other, and mercilessly true.

October and November were joyous days of pacing the floor while dictating to Belle, and evenings reading aloud such stuff that Lloyd could find no words sufficient for its praise. One afternoon he closed the dictation with a happy sigh. "I honestly believe this will be the best thing I've ever done," he said, and went downstairs.

Seldom is it given to an actor to make his exit at the peak of success, but RLS always had said he was lucky. On December 3 everything was good—Charles Baxter was coming to the island for a visit, a collected edition of his works was being oversubscribed, Thanksgiving dinner for some American visitors had gone well. There was no conceivable reason for Fanny to feel depressed. Yet she greeted him with "I have a terrible premonition. Something dreadful has happened, there's a load on my mind I can't lift." Laughing, Louis kissed her gloomy face and, to cheer her up, offered to make a special salad dressing.

Suddenly his hands flew to his head. "Look at me!" he cried. "Do I look strange?" His legs sagged as they helped him to a chair and before the doctor could get to him, he died. His last question was the same he had asked his mother at the age of three.

There were strange things about his death. Though tuberculosis had hung over him for years, he died of a stroke. And the last paragraph in *Weir of Hermiston*, written the day he died, seems to have a special significance: ". . . there arose from before him the curtains of boyhood, and he saw for the first time the ambiguous face of woman as she is . . ." RLS too was emerging from boyhood, he too was at last looking upon woman straightforward, and in this unfinished masterpiece he seems to be embarking on greatness. It is sad that he had to die so early, but it is fine that he died with the light on his face, going forward.

They buried him, as he had wished, on the top of a nearby

hill. His *Requiem* was engraved on a bronze plaque, and many years later Fanny was laid beside him. He who, while lying with his arm strapped to his side, had been able to see his life "a big thing in successes, really," would surely have agreed that he had finished it a very fortunate man.

Rudyard Kipling

(1865=1936)

Rudyard Kipling

(1865=1936)

IN November, 1907, Rudyard Kipling broke one of the iron-bound rules of his life. When the Swedish Academy offered him the Nobel Prize for Literature, the first time any English writer had been so honored, he surprised the world by accepting it. His explanation was that foreign honors, unlike the domestic article, carried no entangling strings, and that his only reason for consistently refusing British decorations or titles had been to leave himself free to criticize his country if he saw fit. "I couldn't rail or snort at the local gods," he said, "if I were wearing their badge."

Here one sees Rudyard Kipling whole, ever his own man and chafing against all shackles. (Except one. "But that," as he would have said, "is another story," a mystery no one was ever allowed to penetrate.)

Few public figures ever fought for their independence and privacy as savagely as he did, entreating future biographers to examine his works rather than his life and covering his tracks so thoroughly that his autobiography does not even mention the name of his wife.

This privacy complex extended to his writings, for unlike most authors, who pop up revealingly from time to time, in all Kipling's thousands of poems, short stories and novels he opened his heart only two or three times. True, he used for material his own colorful environment, but it is a picture without himself among the figures.

His parents were both remarkable people. Lockwood Kipling, scholar, artist and craftsman, had been sent from London to Bombay to run a new art school, and though never wealthy, he was rich in friendships and the deep affection of his family. His wife was one of the five unusual Mac-Donald sisters, of whom two married famous artists, Sir Edward Burne-Jones and Sir Edward Poynter. Another was the mother of Stanley Baldwin, later Prime Minister. Alice MacDonald, Rudyard's mother, was notable in her own right too, blessed with beauty, wit, and a charm that drew all to her in an admiring circle.

India at this time had been for barely seven years a part of the British Empire, and Bombay was a new, progressive city. Railways snaked out across the scorching plains and up into the cooler hills, carrying the British rulers to military posts and burgeoning industrial cities. Here the immediate world of little Rudyard and his sister Trix was the bungalow beside the father's studio, where the boy spoke Hindi before he learned English, and where he ruled the manservant and nurse like a tiny rajah. Lively and boisterous, he visited the native shops and temples with them, absorbing their sights and smells and sounds, and while this was most useful for a future writer, it was less so for a boy doomed shortly to spend six years in a boarding-home for Anglo-Indian exiles.

Since it was thought that no white child could survive the heat of India, the Kiplings bowed to custom and took their own two back to England and put them in the care of a couple in Southsea whose advertisement they had seen in a newspaper. Thinking to ease the separation, the parents gave their children no warning but merely disappeared one dreadful day, leaving them in charge of a woman they were told to address as "Aunty Rosa." Five and three, the deserted youngsters clung to each other in bewilderment and terror.

In Kipling's autobiography, and also in his story "Baa, Baa, Black Sheep," he gives an account of the six years that

RUDYARD KIPLING
(ca. 1900)

followed for himself and Trix with "Aunty Rosa" and "Uncle Harry," her sea captain husband. It is a true horror story of senseless persecution by "The Woman" and her adolescent son, "The Devil-Boy." Aunty Rosa, it appears, was horrified by what her advertisement had brought into her home; in her opinion, children were to be seen and not heard, but this little monster chattered incessantly, asked impertinent questions, and had no idea what orders were for. Worse, although Rudyard was nearly six, he could not even read. So she set him grimly to spelling out "The Cat Lay on the Mat," giving him long passages of the Bible and the prayer book to memorize as penalty for misbehavior. (This served him well, as it happened, for his famous prose style was drenched in the beauties of the King James Version.)

Moreover, he was frequently thrashed. Trix, who was docile and pretty, escaped such treatment and tearfully begged for mercy for him, while The Uncle, as long as he lived, likewise intervened. But when once The Woman and The Devil-Boy were in full control, his life became something out of the Dark Ages. To escape the whip he retreated into lies, which were at once detected and led to the further torture of wearing a placard, LIAR, pinned to his back. In adult life he wryly thanked these two for teaching him a constant wariness of people's moods and tempers, quick footwork, and an automatic suspicion of sudden favors. And it is noticeable that he never again trusted easily. Aunty Rosa and The Devil-Boy were undoubtedly the ones chiefly to blame—but that early abandonment by his parents could not have helped very much.

This affectionate, well-meaning couple had no idea of the damage they had done, for the children, warned of the fate of talebearers, said nothing when they went for their annual holidays to stay with beloved Aunt Georgy Burne-Jones, their mother's sister. It was only when Ruddy nearly went blind from reading in the dark that the situation was brought to light. Then, with no more warning than before, the beautiful mother reappeared. When she entered the room and ran to kiss him, she was puzzled to see him fling up his arm defensively; six years had taught him quick reaction to any sudden moves by grown-ups.

The next year was one of recuperating in the country with his mother and Trix, of learning to play again with his cousin, Stanley Baldwin, to see again with glasses, and to trust again. He seemed to have forgotten the past, and his love for his mother was undoubtedly unimpaired, but many years later he wrote, "When young lips have drunk deep of the bitter waters of Hate, Suspicion and Despair, all the Love in the world will not wholly take away that knowledge." There did seem to be a residue of hate in his sometimes brutal stories and his glorification of war.

Formal schooling began at twelve, when he went to the United Services College at Westward Ho! in Devonshire. Though this was a preparatory school for future army officers, Ruddy, with his bad vision, had no army ambitions. He was sent there solely because the headmaster was "Uncle Crom" Price, beloved family friend and brilliant English teacher. Some of the masters might practice harsh discipline, but Uncle Crom gently fostered Ruddy's originality and talent. It was fortunate soil for such a seedling to fall upon.

At twelve Ruddy was a cheery, capering youngster with a broad grin, bushy brows and deeply cleft chin. His myopic eyes needing no help for reading, he wore his glasses pushed up on his forehead for close work and down on his nose for distance. The boy's early-sprouting moustache produced an exotic aura of world-wisdom disconcerting in one so young.

School was a lonely and bewildering place at first, but soon he found two friends in George Beresford, an Irish boy with a sharp face and tongue to match, and "Stalky" Dunsterville. Beresford's pose was lofty superiority and Ruddy's worldly omniscience. Dunsterville, an artist at "stalking" (performing

Rudyard Kipling

a practical joke without leaving a trace of the perpetrator), was the undercover genius. Mischievous and trying Stalky & Company certainly were, and Kipling's subsequent tales of them are in essence true, but much of the horseplay was a wild exaggeration which he invented in collaboration with a small friend many years later.

Everyone knew Ruddy was to be a writer and, happily exempted by his eyes from sports, he was free to practice his craft unmolested. In his third year Uncle Crom started a school paper, largely with Ruddy's talents in mind, and soon the boy was writing most of its prose and verse, as well as editing, proofreading, and seeing it into print. Not long afterward, he sold an article to a London paper, and, un known to himself, also became the author of a book, for Uncle Crom had sent his verses to his parents, who had them printed privately. The style of the verse was a cross-section of his various literary idols.

Beginning with the Americans, Emerson, Poe, Whitman, Twain and Joel Chandler Harris, and going on to Swinburne, Browning and the Bible, he tried out the mannerisms of each, teaching himself to write in a variety of styles and dialects, and applying himself so thoroughly that at fifteen his literary apprenticeship was finished. Sensing this fact, his father wrote to him from India proposing a newspaper job in Lahore. But by this time there were certain complications, for the young man was in love.

Flo Garrard, a schoolmate of Trix's, was a white-skinned, dark-haired beauty whose childhood abroad had given her a shallow sophistication beyond her sixteen years. There is no record of how often they met or when, but on receipt of his father's proposal he told Beresford, not altogether in jest, that he intended to cable back, "I have married a wife and therefore I cannot come."

Go he did, of course, but the boy that sailed was a man emotionally. Somehow his ardor touched this marble girl a little. His plea for some commitment, some engagement, wrung from her what he took to be a promise, and he in turn left for India utterly committed. In spite of everything, he remained so for many years. Though only a dim presence in the background of his life, Flo Garrard breaks into his story occasionally, always troubling, always giving pain, and if, as some think, she was the model for Maisie in *The Light That Failed*, the portrait is hardly an attractive one.

Rudyard reached Lahore, where his father was principal of the art school and museum, in October, 1882. The city was divided into the English quarter, with bungalows, Punjab Club, schools, colleges and shops, and the Asian quarter, something out of the Arabian Nights with its Mosque of Wazir Khan, its Shalimar Gardens and Tomb of the Emperor Jahangir.

During the summer the heat rose unbearably to ninety-seven degrees at midnight, and cholera, malaria and other tropical diseases spared neither white- nor brown-skinned inhabitant. The only refuge was the Himalayas, known cozily by the English as "The Hills," and there most of them fled for half of every year.

The parents who greeted their sixteen-year-old son were somewhat shaken by his rich whiskers and noisy exuberance, but they took him to their hearts, providing him with bachelor quarters in their bungalow, a manservant, a pony and trap, and coolies to work the ceiling fans day and night. He was introduced at the Punjab Club, where men thrice his age looked with distaste at this young cub who failed to wilt under a snub. An old hand at newspapering, he threw himself joyously into action at the *Civil and Military Gazette*. The *Gazette* shuddered and stood firm.

His salary was six pounds and a half a month, the work never-ending, but, sitting in clinging shirt and trousers in a pool of his own sweat, with glasses slipping off his nose, he was utterly content, even when he was blacked out with fever and had to ask next day what idiot had written his copy. Rudyard's editor found his rush of new ideas somewhat overwhelming, but when the older man was ill, which was often, he was gratified to find his subordinate taking over and running the office with precocious efficiency.

During the hot months, when the family escaped to Simla, seven thousand feet up, Rudyard stayed behind and sweated them out in the silent bungalow. After midnight, when the paper had been put to bed, he wandered the sultry streets, too hot to sleep, and, penetrating where few Europeans dared to go, he absorbed the smells and sights of the Asian quarter. He swapped stories with the laughing, blaspheming soldiers in the army barracks. He talked with the coolies working the fans and learned the ways and thoughts of back-country natives. He listened to middle-aged civil servants drunkenly spilling out the tragedies of their lives. And everything was stored away. Nothing, it was said, ever escaped him after the age of seven.

After he had been in Lahore a couple of years his sister Trix came out from England, and the four Kiplings made up the "Family Square," wherein dwelt affection and mutual respect and from which he received judicious praise and the candid criticism that tidied up his sprawling genius. This was the only audience he cared about pleasing.

Outside the Family Square, back in England, there was forever a grating presence that haunted him. To Flo he wrote and wrote and she answered once or twice, never often enough. Then came one letter too many: it had been two years since he had gone away; he was so young and it would be so long before he could get married; didn't he really think long engagements were a mistake, and would he mind terribly . . .

Savagely he put her behind him and laughed at the thought of caring, persuading himself, in an occasional paragraph dropped into a story, that the whole thing was a joke:

"Next to a requited attachment," he wrote in a juvenile essay, "one of the most convenient things a young man can carry about is an *un*requited attachment. It makes him feel important and businesslike and blasé and cynical; and whenever he has a touch of liver or suffers from want of exercise, he can mourn over his lost love and be very happy in a tender, twilight fashion." All very adult and sophisticated. But still there was the poem, ". . . sudden she crushed the embers 'neath her heel, and all light went with her." Flo was not so easily forgotten, after all.

The Family Square, though, were the ones he loved simply and truly. The months of each year he spent with them in Simla among the Viceroy set groomed him and gave him grace, and the family watched with loving amusement as he learned to ride and dance and pay a compliment. Moreover, they kept him remarkably chaste. Preferring the company of his own three to racier attractions, he contentedly squired the tall and lovely Trix, his "Ice Maiden," to balls and remained his own man.

But one thing neither the Viceroy set nor Lahore's back streets taught him—that there were people in India other than white sahibs and brown servants. An educated middle class of Indians, already gathering volume and power, was in time to become the real nation, but he left the country too early to know that. To him India was always a child of the mother country, England, and a part of the "White Man's Burden." He never understood the condemnation this point of view eventually brought down on him. But that was far in the future, and in the meantime he was to enjoy such popularity as few writers have known.

At twenty-one, bursting with ideas, he was turning out a story a week for his paper. There were tales of Simla society, and of three soldiers in the barracks; there were ghost stories in the manner of Poe, and haunting glimpses of the dim world of the half-caste. For inspiration he needed no more

Rudyard Kipling

than a snatch of gossip at a dance, the whining story of a beggar, an anecdote told at a bar. Exactly a column and a half long, they were cryptic and knowing and sometimes scandalous, and were written in a brand-new conversational style. Often they ended abruptly with a phrase that instantly caught on—"but that's another story."

Following these came longer tales, which were soon republished in six volumes and within a year were on all the railway book stalls. His only problem was to maintain quality in the face of the demand, and it is hardly surprising that the young cub's cockiness became more pronounced than ever.

Then there entered a new influence on his life in the persons of a government meteorologist and his wife. Professor Aleck Hill was a large, burly man with a quiet manner; "Ted," his wife, about thirty, had a face more amusing than beautiful, a snub nose, and dark hair that grew low in a widow's peak. She was American, always laughing and eager for new experiences.

One night the Hills went to a dinner party, and the next day Ted wrote to her younger sister in Beaver, Pennsylvania:

> Opposite me sat a short, dark-haired man with a heavy moustache and very thick glasses. He is beginning to be bald and looks about forty, but really is only twenty-two. He was animation itself, and those near him were kept in gales of laughter. But when more serious topics were discussed, he was posted along those lines too. After dinner, seeking copy perhaps, he came over and began questioning me about my homeland, and I was surprised at his knowledge of people and places. He is worth knowing, and we shall ask him to dinner soon.

The nature of the resulting friendship is an open question. Rudyard dined and rode constantly with both husband and wife, and during his last year in India lived in their house, but it was to the wife that he gave his manuscripts to criticize and wrote long letters when he was away. These letters spoke much of a woman he called "my lady" whom, he implied, he loved without hoping, refusing to name her but leaving an inference to be drawn. Whether this attraction was as strong on her side as on his no one knows. At least her husband continued to be Rudyard's friend and when they decided to visit her family in Pennsylvania, both of them urged him to come along. He could go on to London afterward.

Rudyard once said, "Every card in my working life has been dealt me in such a manner that I had but to play it as it came." At twenty-four he was already a large fish in a small pond and had been getting restless for more challenging waters. The Hills' invitation, therefore, was certainly tempting. Furthermore, an Indian paper offered to take a set of travel sketches to be done during the trip, friends offered introductions all along the route, and a young man named Thomas Cook offered him the use of his travel agency. How could one fail to see how the cards were falling?

In March, 1889, the Hills and Rudyard left Calcutta for Rangoon, Singapore, Hong Kong, Nagasaki, Yokohama and San Francisco. Reaching the Golden Gate, his quick tongue let him in for trouble, for being unused to giving interviews, he made tactless remarks about the local accent, the food, the table manners, the habit of spitting and carrying pistols on the street. "He blazed away at us ferociously," the reporters wrote, and his comments, reprinted all over the country, made him an army of enemies.

Though he soon realized his mistake, he felt that his remarks had been purposely blown up out of malice and, unable ever to forget an injury, he developed a distrust of reporters which was to bring regrettable results later. Actually, he had been enchanted by the Westerners. This appreciation increased as he worked east, so that after a few days in Beaver he was writing lyrically: "Here were Americans, men ruling themselves for themselves and their wives and children, in peace, order and decency, living an absolutely fresh, wholesome and sweet life."

Ted's family he found likewise attractive—her father a college president, her sister Caroline, a girl plump and laughing like herself. After two happy months the party set out again for New York and London. Aleck Hill had already gone on to India and Ted was to rejoin him later, taking Caroline and her brother with her.

The stopover in New York was marred for Rudyard by an experience that, given his particular nature, assumed undue and unhappy importance. He had received from London a sheaf of laudatory reviews: ". . . a more readable and amusing book then *Soldiers Three* we have seldom come across . . ." and ". . . a new literary star is rising in the East." With the clippings and a copy of the book under his arm he called on a prominent editor, hoping for publication in America. After a quick reading, the editor returned the book with a curt, "Young man, this firm is devoted to the publication of *literature*."

His feeling for American publishers was not further sweetened when another one, taking advantage of the muddled copyright situation, issued a pirated version of *Plain Tales from the Hills* without payment of royalty. These two grievances took root and grew and dropped seeds that produced a bitter crop.

The party arrived in London in October, 1889. Though Rudyard had plenty of relatives there, few friends remained after his seven-year absence and, finding his own way around, he took two rooms over the establishment of "Harris the Sausage King" in a building later rechristened Kipling House. The neighborhood was seedy but he could afford no better, having sold nothing in America and being too proud to borrow. Caroline and Ted fluttered around, making housewifely noises, but after three weeks they too were gone.

Little of his relationship with these two women has survived Rudyard's censorship, and though they saved the letters he wrote them, they are hardly revealing. In Beaver, Ted had gently pushed her young courtier toward the more appropriately aged Caroline and he had obediently attached himself. In London he squired her about as finances permitted, and after the two women left for India he wrote them both a few letters, those to Ted chatty and guardedly proper, Caroline's playfully loving, with a few inoffensive endearments such as "heart o' mine." There is some mention of marriage, also. But the proposal, if such it was, was delivered, be it noted, after she had safely left for the other side of the world.

Whatever feeling he had felt for Caroline, however, was extinguished a month later. Walking through the streets of Soho he passed a tall girl with a cloud of dark hair and white marble face. He had not let himself try to learn her whereabouts, but this gift from fate could not be ignored. "Flo!" he cried.

She was as beautiful and distant and haunting as ever, and he was as helpless before her. Though he threw himself on her mercy she was unmoved, interested only in making her name as a painter, and the more he wooed, the further she withdrew. By the beginning of 1890, the crucial year of his life, he was drawn, ill, and deeply dispirited.

One of his poems contains the famous line, "the female of the species is more deadly than the male," and it has been noted that his relationships with women do suggest a fear and distrust of them. Those who analyze such matters have suggested that in the lonely formative years after his parents' abandonment the only woman he knew, the dreaded Aunty Rosa, had given him a loathing of the whole woman-race. Certainly he falls into the pattern of the man who, wounded irrecoverably by one woman, never dares let himself love another—or, unable to resist loving, unconsciously saves himself from too close and dangerous a contact by choosing a woman he can never have. The three he had cared for so far were all inaccessible: Ted Hill was married and thus safely out of reach; Caroline he proposed to only after she had gone out of reach; and Flo simply refused to come within his reach. There was to be one more woman, this one a relationship that mystified all who knew him. The effect of Aunty Rosa may have been at the bottom of that one, too.

Friends, this miserable winter, noted his haggard appearance, and knowing nothing of his anguish worried about his pocketbook and his eating habits. But he was simply living up to his code: the strong suffered in silence, never crying out. And he never did, thrusting grief and pain deep out of sight. Many years later they took a cruel revenge.

Immediately on reaching London, he made his presence known and editors there gave him a warm reception. One Sidney Low, who already knew of his work in India, wrote to a friend:

> One morning there walked into my office a short, dark young man with a bowler hat, a rather shabby tweed coat, a charming smile and, behind specs, a pair of the brightest eyes I had ever seen. He told me he had to make his way in English literature and intended to do it, though at the time he was young, very poor, and in this country quite unknown. I suggested he might write sketches and short stories for me, which suggestion he willingly accepted. At lunch I got him to tell me about places he had seen in India and elsewhere. He was overflowing with ideas and talked with the same abandon and energy with which he wrote. One after another of the lunchers laid down knife and fork, and presently he had half the room for audience, though he was quite unconscious of the attention he evoked. A day or so later he sent me a contribution. . . .

Almost simultaneously Kipling signed a contract for the British publication of his six Indian books. Thus his period of poverty, when he lived on tuppenny breakfasts and relatives' dinners, was over. Two months later he rang a bell loud and clear with "East is East and West is West, and never the twain shall meet." Refusing to trade on fame won in another land, he published the ballad under the pseudonym "Yussuf," but the critics spotted him at once. "The only one with the divine fire writing now," trumpeted the aged Poet Laureate Tennyson, and when the regal *Times* gave to him a whole editorial the Kipling boom was on.

In this year, 1890, writing in a kind of fury—thanks partly to Flo, whom he was trying to drown in ink—he published over eighty stories, numberless poems, and a full-length novel, *The Light That Failed.* He was possessed by something he called his Daemon, a churning power that took over and did the work for him, and he watched it, fascinated, but conscious of danger too. The ideas were flowing too fast, they were running out of control, and when he tried to slow down he found he couldn't. Then his health broke altogether and after an enforced vacation he cabled his father a cryptic message: "Genesis XLV. 9," which, when read in the text, is: "Haste ye, and go up to my father, and say unto him, Thus saith thy son, God hath made me lord of all Egypt; come down unto me; tarry not." Understanding, the parents tarried not but came, and the blessed Family Square surrounded him again.

The year vital to his career, 1890, was vital also to his personal life. It was the year of the Balestiers. Wolcott Balestier was a young American book publisher with an irresistible personality. Slim, sunny and amusing, he was in London to sign up important authors for his firm and to write a novel. His record attests to his charm, for he bowled over the great of London like ninepins. He not only signed up Kipling but persuaded him to collaborate on a novel—Kipling, who needed no collaborator and despised all American publishers!

Wolcott's mother and his two sisters, Caroline and Josephine, had followed him to London to keep his house and help him entertain. One day when Kipling was in the office a young woman entered with some ledgers—the sister Caroline. Short and forceful, with determined eyes and chin, "Carrie" had dedicated her keen mind to Wolcott's career, and on this occasion she had come in to discuss housekeeping bills. Kipling, three years her junior, was introduced. She fixed her sharp eyes on him and thereafter they met frequently, drawn together by their mutual devotion to Wolcott.

The first time Kipling's mother saw Carrie, her eyes took in everything. "That woman is going to marry our Ruddy," she said with a kind of shudder.

After Rudyard and Wolcott had completed their novel, *The Naulahka*, Rudyard, completed exhausted, started off on a trip around the world, while Wolcott went to Germany on business of his own. There he fell ill with typhoid fever and sent for his mother and sisters. Mrs. Balestier and Josephine, seeing his condition, went to pieces, but Carrie, white and efficient, took cha.ge of the dying man and the hysterical women. She sent a wire about her brother's condition to his great friend Henry James.

"I came back from the cemetery," James wrote to the poet and critic Edmund Gosse, "in one of those big black-and-silver coaches with poor concentrated little Carrie, who wanted to talk to me. She is remarkable in her force, her acuteness, capacity and courage, and in the intense, almost manly nature of her emotion. She is a worthy sister of poor dear big-spirited only-by-death-quenched Wolcott, and can face for all three of them everything they will have to meet now."

Carrie had also sent news of Wolcott's illness to Rudyard, who was in Australia on his world trip. Just before Christmas, came a second cable, this one to announce his friend's death. He rushed back to London, making special arrangements all the way, and eight days after his arrival he and Carrie were married.

This was a marriage made less in heaven than in the

Balestier mind. Rudyard rarely spoke of Wolcott after his death, but once he cried out, "He died so suddenly and so far away! We had so much to say to each other and now I have to wait so long to say it." Wolcott had hoped for the marriage and, dying, had, so to speak, willed his sister to his friend. The wedding was inevitable.

It was a bleak little ceremony overshadowed by their grief and an influenza epidemic that felled most of the couple's relatives. Henry James gave the bride away, but commented privately, "I don't in the least understand his marrying her. I don't forecast the future." W. E. Henley, Kipling's editor and friend, was likewise apprehensive; the match was too much like Robert Louis Stevenson's, which had been so ruinous to Henley's friendship with Stevenson: both brides were Americans, small, driving women with noticeable chins and tiny hands and feet; both bore the same name as their husbands' former loves; both were older than their husbands by several years; and both became their husbands' managers, guardians, housekeepers and inseparable companions.

Rudyard's announcement to Henley of his marriage was as bleak as the wedding: "I don't as a rule let men into any part of life outside the working section, but methinks you are entitled to know that I have this day married Miss Balestier, the sister of the man with whom I wrote *The Naulahka.*"

When Carrie had packed her mother and Josephine off to Vermont and wound up Wolcott's affairs, the couple set off on their honeymoon. Rudyard was trying once again to get around the world, and was once again frustrated, this time by a catastrophe that he took in remarkably good humor. He had deposited two thousand pounds in a London bank with worldwide branches, and one morning in Yokohama he went to draw out ten pounds.

"Why don't you draw out more, Mr. Kipling?" said the manager. "It is just as easy."

Rudyard, failing to notice the man's strained expression,

said, "Oh, I don't like carrying large sums of money. But I'll look over my account and perhaps come back this afternoon." When he did he found the bank closed. It had failed and his money was gone.

They had approximately fifteen pounds in pocket and a child on the way, but with the steamship company's refund and a hundred dollars sent from New York they were able to laugh off the emergency. Besides, they were not sorry to cut short the trip, for when they had stopped in Vermont on the way out Kipling had fallen in love with the place and leased some land from Carrie's brother, Beatty. Now they could go back there and settle down.

These fruitful Vermont years, Rudyard always said, were "blessed to him forever." Only twenty-five when he started building the mountainside mansion named "The Naulahka" in honor of Wolcott, he was soon receiving royalties that made possible an opulent way of living, with imported English servants and a liveried coachman. Some of their Brattleboro neighbors wondered at the local girl who now dressed for dinner so grandly, but Rudyard's charm, though never cozy, won the town. Too, they were both attractive, for nothing is more winning than happiness, and with the birth in 1892 of their daughter Josephine, whom they adored, and the arrival of Rudyard's beloved father, life was indeed blessed. Lockwood Kipling was his son's critic, counselor and friend, and in the long winter evenings they sat, feet on fender and pipes in hand, talking and retalking the jungle lore that went into the Indian stories.

All this worked to the return of the blessed Daemon, who took charge and produced an amazing harvest, *The Just So Stories, Captains Courageous, The Day's Work, Kim* and *The Jungle Books*. It was very gratifying, and almost too easy.

Presently over this demi-paradise a cloud began to float, at first no bigger than a sparrow's shadow. If he and Carrie had been more informal and neighborly it might have passed without harm, but they insisted on privacy, and Carrie stood off, with a high hand, autograph-seekers and reporters. Brattleboro found it hard to stomach this local woman with her English airs. In addition, a dispute between Great Britain and the United States over a faraway Venezuelan border was whipping up anti-British feelings in America. Altogether, it was a poor time to stage a squabble with a local boy.

More unfortunate, the local boy was Carrie's own brother, the tippling, handsome pet of Brattleboro, whose pretty wife was equally convivial. Gifted with the social grace Carrie lacked, Beatty was nevertheless a weakling, and she showed him that she knew it. Engaging him to oversee building jobs on the place, she paid him well enough but doled out the dollars like a child's allowance, and like a child he sulked. Finally his resentment broke into flame and for many months the two couples did not speak.

In March, 1896, soon after the birth of the Kiplings' daughter Elsie, Beatty went into bankruptcy, noisily blaming his sister and Rudyard. Carrie offered to bail him out on one condition—that he stay sober and get a job, preferably out of town. Moreover, she offered to take his child and bring her up decently. At this there was an outburst of rage, and the newspapers got the story.

Rudyard, dogged by reporters, could do nothing but roar at them, "I decline to be interviewed. It is an outrage to be insulted on the public highways and asked the details of one's private life." Then, reverting to his ancient grievance, he thundered, "Your American copyright laws have already swindled me out of considerable money. Is it not enough to steal my books without intruding on my private life?"

The final eruption came on a country road, when Beatty charged down upon Rudyard and yelled, "See here, I want to talk to you."

Like ice Rudyard replied, "If you have anything to say, see my lawyer."

Rudyard Kipling

"You damned conceited English scribbler," Beatty shouted, "you've been lying about me all over town, saying I can't bring up my own child, that you've been holding me up by the seat of my pants. Apologize, do you hear? Apologize!" Rudyard glared in silence, and he went on, "If you don't take it back within a week, I'll blow your brains out!"

"You'll kill me, is that it?" asked Rudyard, low and level. "By God, yes, I will."

"Then," said Rudyard, "you will have only yourself to blame for the consequences." He turned and went home, while Beatty charged off in the opposite direction.

Surely, thought their friends, these two grown men could not mean this absurd scene, surely they would start laughing any minute. But neither wife was amused, and the next day the Kiplings made the blunder of their lives. Rudyard went into court and charged Beatty with threatening to murder him. Beatty was arrested.

Truly, here was disaster, for Beatty, let out on bail, assembled forty reporters in his home and fed them his story over drinks. At the hearing every undignified detail was aired, Beatty and his wife homey and laughing, Rudyard and Carrie coldly furious. The total result was a vague court order bidding Beatty to "keep the peace" and leaving him free to sell his story for a goodly sum. Afterwards Rudyard and Carrie retired, bruised and humiliated, to the silence of The Naulahka. "These are dark days for us," Carrie said. "Rudyard is dull, listless and weary."

Nationwide, the newspapers revealed a hostility that stunned them both. They did not think of their return to England soon after as flight, expecting it to be only a visit, for indeed The Naulahka was still home to them all. But they never returned, for this had been the first serious shock to Rudyard, whose hand till now had had such a sure grasp on events. Secretly he was ashamed, and on arriving in England he seemed to his friends a shade less confident, even a shade bewildered.

239

They took a house in the country, then another, for some years trying out places for comfort and privacy, and periodically they visited London, where the Vermont farce had left his reputation unimpaired. Having lived at an outpost of the British Empire, he was now at the heart of it and delighted in the companionship of prime ministers and dukes. Imperialism at this time was a glorious thing, the possession of colonies an enviable one. Even the British-American rift over colonialism was healing as the United States fought Spain for Cuba and the Philippines and suddenly found herself beside Britain in the colonial camp. Notwithstanding his personal feuds, Kipling admired the United States, seeing the two Anglo-Saxon nations as predestined leaders of the world, and in such writings as "The White Man's Burden" he exhorted them to accept their responsibilities along with the glory.

The theme of Empire, its duties and responsibilities, inspired the poem many regard as his finest. When Queen Victoria celebrated her Diamond Jubilee, Rudyard, as the Empire's unofficial voice, was pressed for an ode, and though he rarely wrote to order, this time he shut himself up to think. At first only one line occurred to him, "lest we forget . . ."— a sound not of exultation but of warning. He could get no further for two weeks, then a few more rough ideas came and he jotted them down.

About this time Rudyard's Aunt Georgy and an American girl, Sallie Norton, were visiting the Kiplings, and one day all four were chatting in Rudyard's study while he cleaned out his desk.

"What are those things you're throwing away?" asked Sallie. "May I look?" She fished a paper out of the basket. Reading, she cried, "Why, you can't throw this out. This has to be published."

"Oh, it's not good enough," he grunted.

"It's magnificent. Let Aunt Georgy look."

Rudyard Kipling

Aunt Georgy agreed vehemently. Overborne, he sat down to polish the material. Sallie suggested repetition of the couplet, "Lord God of Hosts, Be with us yet, Lest we forget, lest we forget," and making the change, he scribbled underneath, "Done in council, July 16, 1897 . . . Aunt Georgy, Sallie, Carrie and me." Thus was "Recessional" written. It is a prayer that earthly power should neither corrupt man nor blind him to a higher Power.

"Recessional" was at one extreme of his range. At the other were the children's stories, revealing his gentle delight in all children, especially in his own three: Josephine, the blue-eyed six-year-old; Elsie, the grinning toddler; and the baby, John. With companionable little Josephine he explored the countryside, reciting her favorite verses and making up stories as they walked. They were the original Taffimai and Tegumai, and their discussions about the How and Why of things became the *Just So Stories*.

Everything Josephine wanted was also his wish for her. "My little maid is altogether a little American," he said, "and she wants to go home." So, with Carrie's mother in Vermont, and the need to attend to some American copyright business supplying the excuse, they sailed for the United States in February, 1899.

The voyage was rough and upsetting, and the children came down with whooping cough a few days after they arrived. Then Carrie fell ill. All recovered and they were soon out sightseeing. Two weeks later, Rudyard developed pneumonia and Josephine followed suit. Carrie, none too well herself, took full charge.

Many years afterward, Elsie Kipling admitted that her mother had been jealous, possessive, sharp-tempered and overbearing, but she recognized her never-failing courage. This courage was never so apparent as in the next month. With her husband ill in a New York hotel and the two younger children down again with whooping cough, Carrie took the weakening Josephine to friends on Long Island and, assisted by nurses, cared for the others. Downstairs, the detested reporters clamored for news. Beatty chose this moment to threaten a lawsuit.

Rudyard's pneumonia deepened daily, and in delirium he wandered the world searching for Robert Louis Stevenson or galloping with armies across the steppes of Central Asia. Meantime, crowds blocked the traffic outside, while prayers were offered for him in churches and some even knelt on the hotel steps. His doctors could only say that they were "not without hope." At last the fever broke and the danger was over.

Telegrams of rejoicing poured in, only to stop in shocked embarrassment, for frail little Josephine was not shaking off her illness. Carrie, leaving Rudyard for one day, went out to see her and that night wrote in her diary: "March 5. I saw Josephine three times today, morning, afternoon, and at ten P.M. for the last time. She was conscious for a moment and sent her love to 'Daddy and all.'" With that intense manly courage noted by Henry James, she made another stiff entry next day: "March 6. Josephine left us at 6:30 this morning."

With Rudyard only recently out of danger, his doctors feared to have him told of Josephine's death. Carrie, returning from the funeral to his room and remembering too late the black dress she was wearing, flung a bright red shawl around her shoulders and went in to him with a smile.

In time he learned, of course, and in time he recovered—physically. Of him his cousin, Angela Thirkell, said, "There was the same charm as before, the same gift of fascinating speech and way of making everyone show his most interesting side. But there was always a barrier after that." He and Carrie simply pulled together a little closer, and in gratitude he wrote to her mother:

> You have no notion what a sweet and winning little woman your Carrie has grown into. Her face gets more beautiful year by year, and her character deepens and

broadens with every demand upon it. She is near an angel, but her Puritan conscience, which she has inherited from her New England forebears, makes her take life too blame seriously.

The significant words are, "has grown into," and the deliberately light "too blame seriously." That wariness as to moods and tempers he had learned from Aunty Rosa had been useful and necessary all these years.

The heartache of Josephine's death, like that of Flo Garrard, he sought to drown in work. *Stalky & Co.* appeared now to the delight of those intrigued by something autobiographical. Then there occurred an event large enough to distract him completely—Britain's war in South Africa. Taking the family to Capetown, he wrote patriotic songs, visited hospitals, raised funds. There he became a close friend of Cecil Rhodes, the diamond millionaire who had developed the country of Rhodesia. Rhodes put a house at their disposal, and during the following seven winters the two men planned the famous Rhodes Scholarships, designed to develop leaders in England and America. There too Rudyard helped Sir Robert Baden-Powell plan the Boy Scout movement, whose wolf-cubs were named for *The Jungle Book's* Mowgli.

When peace came in 1902 the Kiplings retired to the English countryside and the final perfect home, "Bateman's," a three-hundred-year-old farmhouse surrounded by thirty Sussex acres. Though only thirty-six, his prestige and wealth made him seem almost an elder statesman, and during the following decade he gave much of his thought to politics and world affairs. He warned of Germany's growing might and ambitions and of her preparations for submarine warfare; he warned of Russia, "the bear that walks like a man"; he warned England against her unpreparedness and called for universal military service. But, elder statesman though he was, England did not listen. In 1914 his fears were realized. World War I broke out.

His son John was by now almost seventeen, a tall, slight, humorous lad who, rejected at first for military service on account of bad eyesight and varicose veins, was helped by Rudyard's influence to get into a crack British regiment. On his eighteenth birthday, August 17, 1915, he left for the front, taken by his parents and Elsie to the train. In silence they watched as he walked away and then turned, straight and tall and pitifully young, to give them a smart salute. That was the last time they ever saw him.

Less then two months later the name of Lieutenant John Kipling appeared in the casualty lists: "Wounded and missing in action." For two years they hoped, Carrie praying he had been taken prisoner, and Trix, whose mind was already unsteadily balanced, slipping away into the beyond in search of his spirit. Rudyard grimly shook his head, for he had seen war at first hand and while he might hope, he would not fool himself. Finally they met a man who had seen John fall, shot through the head.

Carrie was prostrated. Rudyard suffered doubly, remembering that the boy, once rejected, need never have gone to war except for him. His influence had blasted open the way; moreover, he had so glorified soldiering, trumpeting a call for universal service, that there had been nothing else the son could do. The broken man hid his grief in the silence of Bateman's.

The following years were shaken by more than grief. Rudyard Kipling, so long the prophet and leader, with a clear eye and a sure touch, now found that his hand had truly lost its grasp. Far to the political right, he stood fixed while England moved away from him, and this time when he warned against events they failed to prove him right. Empire and the White Man's Burden were out of style. The last years saw him stubbornly clinging to a position no longer tenable.

His frustration and unexpressed grief took their toll in agonizing stomach ulcers. For a long time the cause of his

Rudyard Kipling

suffering was not recognized, such things being less well understood then than now, and he could only hide this pain along with the rest of his suffering.

In a speech at St. Andrews University he had once summed up his creed: "At any price, *let me own myself*, let me always be true to my beliefs." Harsh though he might be and sometimes woefully wrong, this he always was. For better or worse, he believed in the Empire. Upon his death in 1936, two days after the death of his friend George V, the papers said truly, "The King has died and taken his trumpeter with him."

But it was not the trumpeter who lives on, whose books keep making new friends year after year. It was the chronicler of Mowgli and Kim and Rikki-Tikki-Tavi, the young father who walked with his little girl and told her stories of the How and Why of things.

Bibliography

I. William Shakespeare

A Life of Shakespeare, Hesketh Pearson. London: Carroll & Nicholson, 1949.

Shakespeare of London, Marchette Chute. New York: E. P. Dutton & Co., 1949.

William Shakespeare, A Biography, Alfred L. Rowse. London: Macmillan & Co., Ltd., 1963.

II. Jane Austen

Presenting Miss Jane Austen, May Lamberton Becker. New York: Dodd, Mead & Co., 1952.

Introductions to Jane Austen, John C. Bailey. London: Oxford Univ. Press, 1931.

Memoir of Jane Austen, James E. Austen-Leigh. Oxford: Clarendon Press, 1926.

Jane Austen, Elizabeth Jenkins. New York: Farrar, Straus and Cudahy, 1949.

Jane Austen: Facts and Problems, Robert W. Chapman. Oxford: Clarendon Press, 1948.

Jane Austen, Her Life and Letters, Wm. and R. A. Austen-Leigh. London: Smith, Elder, 1913.

"Love and Friendship" and Other Early Works by Jane Austen, Preface by Gilbert K. Chesterton. New York: Frederick A. Stokes Co., 1922.

Bibiography

III. NATHANIEL HAWTHORNE

The Inward Sky: The Mind and Heart of Nathaniel Hawthorne, Hubert H. Hoeltje. Durham, N. C.: Duke Univ. Press, 1962.

Nathaniel Hawthorne, A Biography, Randall Stewart. New Haven: Yale Univ. Press, 1948.

Hawthorne, Mark Van Doren. New York: Viking Press, 1962.

Hawthorne, Newton Arvin. New York: Russell & Russell, 1961.

The Life and Genius of Nathaniel Hawthorne, Frank P. Stearns. Philadelphia & London: J. B. Lippincott Co., 1906.

Nathaniel Hawthorne, A Modest Man, Edward Mather (Pseudonym). New York: Thomas Y. Crowell Co., 1940.

IV. EDGAR ALLAN POE

Israfel: The Life and Times of Edgar Allan Poe, Hervey Allen. New York: Geo. H. Doran Co., 1927.

The Haunted Palace, A Life of Edgar Allan Poe, Frances Winwar. New York: Harper, 1959.

V. CHARLES DICKENS

Charles Dickens, His Character, Comedy and Career, Hesketh Pearson. New York: Harper, 1949.

Life of Charles Dickens, John Forster. London: Chapman & Hall, 1872.

Charles Dickens, Gilbert K. Chesterton. London: Methuen & Co., 1906.

Eight Essays, Edmund Wilson. Garden City: Doubleday, 1954.

The Man Charles Dickens, A Victorian Portrait, E. C. Wagenknecht. Boston & New York: Houghton, Mifflin Co., 1929.

VI. THE BRONTËS

Charlotte Brontë, Edward F. Benson. London: Longmans, Green & Co., 1932.

Passionate Search, A Life of Charlotte Brontë, Margaret Crompton. New York: David McKay Co., 1955.

The Life of Charlotte Brontë, Mrs. Elizabeth Gaskell. New York: D. Appleton & Co., 1857.

Bibiography

Psychoanalyses of the Character and Genius of Emily Brontë, Lucile Dooley. Psychoanalytic Review, Vol. 17, 1930.

Study of the Novels of Charlotte and Emily Brontë, Harold G. McCurdy. Character and Personality, December, 1947.

The Brontë Story, Margaret Lane. New York: Duell, Sloan & Pearce, 1953.

VII. JULES VERNE

Jules Verne, A Biography of an Imagination, George H. Waltz, Jr. New York: Henry Holt & Co., 1943.

Jules Verne, Kenneth Allott. London: The Cresset Press, 1940.

Jules Verne, Marguerite Allotte De La Fuÿe. London: Staples Press, 1954.

VIII. MARK TWAIN

America's Own Mark Twain, Jeanette Eaton. New York: Wm. Morrow, 1958.

Mark Twain's Autobiography, Edited by Charles Neider. New York: Harper, 1959.

Life on the Mississippi, Mark Twain. New York: Harper & Bros., 1917.

Enchantment, Dorothy Quick. Norman: Univ. of Oklahoma Press, 1961.

Mark Twain Himself: A Pictorial Biography, Milton Meltzer. New York: Thomas Y. Crowell, 1960.

Roughing It, Mark Twain. New York: Harper & Bros., 1899.

IX. ROBERT LOUIS STEVENSON

Stevensoniana, John A. Hammerton. Edinburgh: J. Grant, 1910.

The Stevensons: Louis and Fanny, Laura L. Hinkley. New York: Hastings House, 1950.

Voyage to Windward, The Life of Robert Louis Stevenson, Joseph C. Furnas. New York: Wm. Sloane Associates, 1951.

The True Stevenson. A Study in Clarification, George S. Hellman. Boston: Little Brown & Co., 1925.

Robert Louis Stevenson, Gilbert K. Chesterton. London: Hodder and Stoughton, Ltd., 1927.

Bibiography

The Strange Case of Robert Louis Stevenson, Malcolm Elwin. London: Macdonald, 1950.

Last Witness for Robert Louis Stevenson, Elsie Noble Caldwell. Norman: Univ. of Oklahoma Press, 1960.

Tusitala of the South Seas, Joseph Waldo Ellison. New York: Hastings House, 1953.

Lay Morals, and Other Papers, Robert Louis Stevenson. London: Chatto & Windus, 1911.

X.   RUDYARD KIPLING

Rudyard Kipling: A Study in Literature and Political Ideas, Edward Shanks. London: Macmillan & Co., Ltd., 1940.

Rudyard Kipling, A New Appreciation, Hilton Brown. London: H. Hamilton, 1945.

Something of Myself, For My Friends Known and Unknown, Rudyard Kipling. Garden City: Doubleday, Doran & Co., 1937.

Rudyard Kipling, At Home and At Work, D. Ponton. Poole, Dorset: Printed by J. Looker, 1953.

The Wound and The Bow: Seven Studies In Literature, Edmund Wilson. Boston: Houghton Mifflin Co., 1941.

Rudyard Kipling, A Friendly Profile, Lucile R. Carpenter. Chicago: Argus Books, 1942.

Life of Rudyard Kipling, Charles E. Carrington. Garden City: Doubleday, 1925.

920
ST1

780

Stirling, Nora
Who wrote the classics?

DATE			
MAY 7 ᴿᴱ '84			